Norton

Norton

A Racing Legend

Jim Reynolds

CHARTWELL
BOOKS, INC.

A QUINTET BOOK

Published by Chartwell Books
A Division of Book Sales, Inc.
PO box 7100
Edison, New Jersey 08818-7100

This edition produced for sale in the U.S.A.,
its territories and dependencies only.

ISBN 0-7858-0310-6

This book was designed and produced by
Quintet Publishing Limited
6 Blundell Street
London N7 9BH

Creative Director: Richard Dewing
Designer: Simon Balley
Senior Project Editor: Stefanie Foster
Text Editor: Kit Coppard

Typeset in Great Britain by
Central Southern Typesetters, Eastbourne
Manufactured by Regent Publishing Services Ltd, China
Printed by Leefung Asco Printers Ltd, China

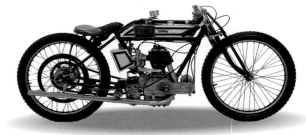

Contents

CHAPTER ONE

THE SIDE-VALVERS

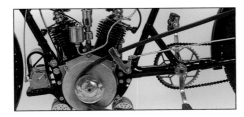

*E*arly motorcycles were crude machines, using only established technology to guarantee reliability. Norton's products were solid, well-made, and essentially simple, in a world where the public was still being persuaded that the internal combustion engine was to be relied upon in the long term. James Norton cautiously used other makers' engines in the early years, then moved on to develop his own power units in the light of experience. Side valves served him well.

JAMES LANSDOWNE NORTON, a man of high principles, gave his name to one of the great legends of motorcycling. The Norton name grew from humble beginnings to be known all over the world to many millions for high-quality machines and a great racing heritage.

James Norton was born in Birmingham, England, in 1869, the son of a cabinetmaker and clearly very bright from his early years. When he was only ten, he built a model steam engine that had crowds gathering in the street when he set it running in the front parlor window. After school he was apprenticed to the jewelry trade, where some of Birmingham's finest craftsmen were trained, but in 1898 he recognized the growing interest in bicycles and set up on his own, forming the Norton Manufacturing Company. From premises in Bradford Street, in the center of the growing city, he operated as a "supplier of parts and fittings to the cycle trade," producing frame lugs and complete frames as well as chains. A committed member of the Salvation Army, he recruited youngsters from the Army's Citadel in nearby Sparkbrook to work on cycle assembly on Saturdays.

The early powered bikes

The business of building pedal cycles logically led on to motorcycles in the pioneer years at the turn of the century, as makers experimented with crude engines bolted into their frames. James Norton struck up a relationship with Charles Garrard, the British agent for French-built Clément engines, and by 1902 Norton's advertisement for his "Energette" motorcycle ". . . for Business, Touring or Racing" gave the company address as The Garrard Depot in Birmingham's Bromsgrove Street. Among the variations on this Clément-Garrard powered model, Norton offered a Ladies' Model and also claimed to build "the Ideal Doctor's Bike."

▶ JAMES NORTON'S COMPACT LAYOUT WON APPROVAL FROM SOME UNUSUAL SOURCES. THE *JOURNAL OF COMMERCE* WROTE IN 1904: "SINCE THE FIRST DAYS OF BICYCLE MANUFACTURE THE NORTON COMPANY HAVE GIVEN SPECIAL ATTENTION TO ALL IMPROVEMENTS."

▲ THE FIRST NORTON WAS THE "ENERGETTE," POWERED BY A CLEMENT-GARRARD ENGINE AND WITH ALL THE CONTROLS MOUNTED ON THE FUEL TANK. ON THE UNSURFACED ROADS OF THE EARLY 1900S, TAKING YOUR HANDS OFF THE HANDLEBARS TO PUMP OIL TO THE ENGINE WAS THE ACTION OF A BRAVE MAN.

◄ H. REMBRANDT FOWLER
(WITH GOGGLES) LOOKS
REMARKABLY FIT AFTER
WINNING THE TWIN CYLINDER
CLASS IN THE 1907 TT. NEXT
TO HIM, THE BEARDED JAMES
NORTON IS JUSTLY PROUD OF
THE BIKE'S RELIABILITY.

Norton moved up from the small Clément-Garrard units to a Peugeot V-twin for the 1907 season and showed it first at an exhibition in Birmingham's Bingley Halls. It was there that he met H. Rem Fowler, a local enthusiast who was keen to talk to a manufacturer about a bike for new Tourist Trophy races to be held on the Isle of Man that summer. Fowler bought one of the new Peugeot-powered Nortons, and James Norton agreed to act as his pit attendant and give advice and help at the races, to be held around a 15¾ mile triangular course on the western side of the island between the villages of St. John's (starting point), Kirkmichael, and Peel.

First TT victory

It is difficult today to appreciate just how rough conditions were for those racers of 1907, over rural, unpaved lanes that were sprayed with an acid solution to seal in the dust. A few days after the race, Fowler's suit and gloves were full of holes! His ride was certainly not easy, and he fell off when his front inner tube burst; he replaced it and carried on, setting the fastest lap of the race at 42.9mph, winning the twin-cylinder class, and coming third behind Charlie Collier (Matchless) and Jack Marshall (Triumph) on single-cylinder machines.

Fowler described James Norton's contribution as mainly a frantic waving to remind him to operate the hand oil-pump to keep the motor sweet. That historic win set a theme that was to feature throughout Norton's history, and they regarded the TT as the premier proving ground for their machines for the next 50 years. That 1907 event certainly lived up to its Tourist Trophy name, with twin-cylinder bikes required to average at least 75 miles to the gallon. Fowler's Norton actually achieved 87mpg. He described his machine in a letter as "my unapproachable Norton," a phrase taken up and used by the company for years to come.

▲ THE NARROW ANGLE PEUGEOT VEE-TWIN ENGINE GAVE FLEXIBLE POWER AND A TOP SPEED CLOSE TO 60MPH. SOON AFTER HIS TT WIN, REM FOWLER WON A SLOW RACE ON THE MACHINE, WITH THE GEARING UNALTERED.

▼ THE 1907 TT WINNER IS HARDLY A SPEED MACHINE TO MODERN EYES. THE PEDALING GEAR WAS NEEDED TO HELP IT UP THE STEEPEST HILLS ON THE TT COURSE, WHERE HELPERS COULD RUN ALONGSIDE THE RIDERS AND TELL THEM HOW THEY WERE DOING IN THE RACE.

NORTON'S EARLY REPUTATION FOR SPEED WAS FURTHERED BY MEN LIKE REX JUDD (LEFT), WHO WAS THE IDEAL BUILD FOR A RIDER, AND VICTOR HORSMAN (CENTER) WHO TUNED AND RODE HIS OWN MACHINE. D. R. O'DONOVAN (SEATED) TOOK MANY RECORDS HIMSELF BEFORE CONCENTRATING ON TUNING.

JAMES NORTON AGED SO EARLY THAT HIS FATHER, HERE IN THE SIDECAR OF A BIG FOUR OUTFIT IN 1921, WAS OFTEN THOUGHT TO BE HIS BROTHER. JAMES'S HEALTH WAS FAILING AND WITHIN FIVE YEARS HE WAS DEAD.

First Norton engines

The TT class win put Norton firmly in the public eye, and for the 1908 season they offered their own engines, a V-twin and a single. The single-cylinder model featured in their advertisements — a sign of the trend toward the simpler model in years to come, and the V-twin was dropped from the line after a short run. The single featured an 82mm bore and 90mm stroke in its early years, but by 1912 there had been changes and the 490cc model measured 79mm bore x 100mm stroke, while its 633cc Big 4 brother measured 82mm x 120mm.

THE 633CC BIG FOUR, REGARDED AS JAMES NORTON'S FAVORITE MODEL IN THE EARLY DAYS OF THE COMPANY, WAS OFFERED AS A SIDECAR MACHINE AND COULD BE SUPPLIED WITH FOOTBOARDS FOR EXTRA COMFORT.

The Shelley takeover

The Big 4 was James Norton's personal favorite, normally ridden with a sidecar attached and used to test new ideas; he also used a Big 4 when he toured South Africa in the early 1920s. His habit of testing developments himself affected the commercial side, and production would be stopped if "Pa" Norton found a better part, so that the improvement could be incorporated as soon as possible. By 1913 this perfectionist approach took its toll: the Norton Manufacturing Company went into liquidation and was bought by the engineering business R. T. Shelley. The Norton factory was later moved to a building across the road from the Shelley works in Aston Brook Street. The front entrance to the new factory was in Bracebridge Street – an address that was to become famous all over the world as the traditional home of Norton.

The Brooklands connection

With the Shelley involvement came Bob Shelley's brother-in-law, the Brooklands record-breaker and tuner D. R. O'Donovan. He was the driving force behind Norton's many world records on the famous Surrey speed bowl, and he developed the

BS (Brooklands Special) model that was supplied with a certificate stating that it had achieved a speed of 75mph at Brooklands; the alternative version was the BRS (Brooklands Road Special) with a certificated top speed of 70mph. With the rudimentary brakes of the day, a single-gear transmission with no clutch, rigid rear frame, and no more than two inches of travel from the girder front forks, a speed potential of 70mph on the road was quite awesome.

O'Donovan's testing of all the engines in these high-speed models was done at Brooklands, where a batch of engines would be prepared and then

fitted into a chassis kept in his factory for the job of running the engines against the clock to check their speed. The rolling chassis was later fitted permanently with an engine and is now at the National Motor Museum in Beaulieu (in Hampshire, England). It is ridden by selected – and very skillful – riders in the annual Pioneer Run from London to Brighton. With minimal brakes and no clutch, it is no easy ride and certainly not a slow one!

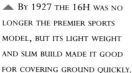 BY 1927 THE 16H WAS NO LONGER THE PREMIER SPORTS MODEL, BUT ITS LIGHT WEIGHT AND SLIM BUILD MADE IT GOOD FOR COVERING GROUND QUICKLY.

► O'DONOVAN'S "OLD MIRACLE" IN ITS WORKING CLOTHES. NOTHING FANCY, THE ABSOLUTE MINIMUM OF EQUIPMENT WITH NO FRONT BRAKE AND A SINGLE GEAR. 80MPH ON SUCH A MACHINE OVER THE BUMPS OF BROOKLANDS MUST HAVE BEEN A STIRRING EXPERIENCE.

◄ WORLD SPEEDWAY CHAMPION BARRY BRIGGS REACHES BRIGHTON SEAFRONT ON THE NATIONAL MOTOR MUSEUM'S "OLD MIRACLE," THE "SLAVE MACHINE" IN WHICH D. R. O'DONOVAN TESTED ENGINES AT BROOKLANDS.

THE BROOKLANDS ROAD SPECIAL (BRS)

Introduced to the line in 1913, the BRS was the road-going version of the BS Brooklands Special racing model. The spindly 490cc side-valve looks slow to the modern eye, but it had been developed by rider-tuner D. R. O'Donovan and came complete with a certificate stating that it had been timed at 70mph at Brooklands. It was the outstanding sports machine of its time and a favorite with sports riders, who were impressed by O'Donovan's speed of 81mph for the flying-start kilometer on a specially tuned BS.

ENGINE Air-cooled vertical single-cylinder with side valves of nickel steel operated by non-adjustable tappets. 79mm bore x 100mm stroke = 490cc. Brown & Barlow carburetor; CAV magneto ignition.

TRANSMISSION Optional direct-belt drive or Phillipson adjustable mainshaft pulley; later, optional Armstrong three-speed hub gear, with ratios of 5.0, 7.5, and 11.3 to 1.

FRAME Norton-built lugged and brazed type. Norton Druid girder front forks.

SUSPENSION Druid front forks providing approx. 2in (51mm)

movement; rear frame rigid.

WHEELS 26in (660mm) rims, 2.5in (64mm) wide Clincher tires. Pedal-operated linkage to block on belt rim as rear brake; stirrup type on rim at front.

EQUIPMENT Lyco padded seat; twin toolboxes on rear carrier; tubular rear stand; straight-through exhaust.

PERFORMANCE Warranted 70mph (113km/h) top speed.

PRICE (1913) £60; Phillipson Pulley £4 extra.

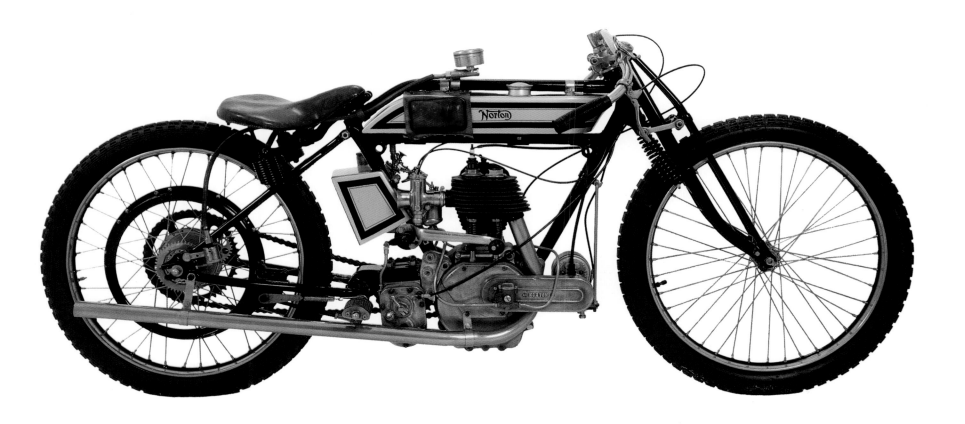

▶ IN 1926 THE 16H WAS THE BEST SELLER, AND CAME FULLY EQUIPPED WITH TOOL BAGS AND REAR CARRIER. FRONT FORKS WERE DRUIDS, BUT HARD RIDERS PREFERRED WEBBS.

▼ VICTOR HORSMAN BROKE NUMEROUS RECORDS AT BROOKLANDS. HE RODE IN THE ISLE OF MAN TT IN 1920 AND 1921, BUT DID NOT FIGURE IN THE RESULTS.

Speed records

The 79mm x 100mm measurements of the 490cc engine stayed with the company for many years, and the earliest versions were the outstanding sports models of their day. Norton's advertisements carried lists of sporting successes and the latest batch of speed records broken at Brooklands, where the more canny professionals beat the previous figure by a modest amount so that they earned bonuses from trade suppliers, but left the new record within reach for the next attempt. Beat the record by 1mph and you could earn five bonuses; beat it once by 5mph, and you only earned one. In 1915 O'Donovan's world

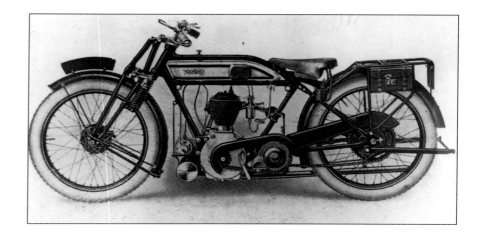

500cc speed record was beaten by a Swiss rider on a Motosacoche. Within a week of hearing the news, he wheeled out one of his faithful Nortons and set a new speed at 82.85mph, using what the company adverts claimed was "an absolutely standard engine." Few can have believed that – but it was still a very impressive speed.

The 490cc side-valve road model was supplied in 16H (Home market) form and 17C (Colonial) form, with higher ground clearance. The 16H stayed in the range for over 40 years, though its status changed during its long life from a sports model in the early 1920s to a mild-mannered and much heavier tourer by the late 1930s. By 1935 the factory realised the vast potential of a machine purpose-built for military use, and a specially prepared 16H was submitted, with other models' for testing by the Mechanical Warfare Experimental Establishment. Their report in December that year said: "Of the 500cc machines, the best is the Norton . . .". In a test carried out over thousands of miles of road and cross-country courses, the 16H won the competition to become the standard British Army motorcycle. The choice was justified, and the model proved itself to be up to any sort of terrain.

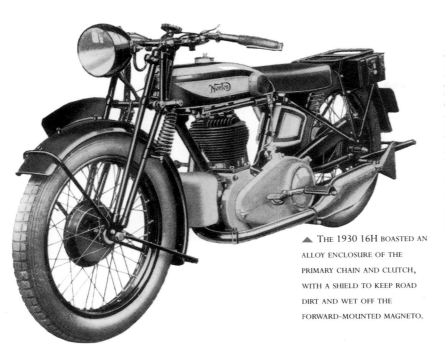

▲ THE 1930 16H BOASTED AN ALLOY ENCLOSURE OF THE PRIMARY CHAIN AND CLUTCH, WITH A SHIELD TO KEEP ROAD DIRT AND WET OFF THE FORWARD-MOUNTED MAGNETO.

Army bikes

By 1939 the factory was concentrating on production of the 16H in its military form, with all other models taking a lower priority. Even racing, in which Norton had become a dominant force, took a back seat as the company geared up for the demands of the British War Department. When war was declared in 1939, the humble 16H in military trim and the Big 4 sidecar outfit were the only models built, and the pressures on production built up. Two inspectors from the War Department were based at the factory, with the authority to inspect any aspect of the work. They once criticized engine timer "Pop" Swinnerton,

◁ THE SOLID AND SIMPLE 16H WAS THE STANDARD MILITARY MACHINE WHEN WORLD WAR TWO BROKE OUT. THE FACTORY MADE 100,000 OF THEM, AND THEY SURVIVED EVERYTHING FROM ICE AND SNOW TO THE HEAT AND SAND OF THE AFRICAN DESERTS.

SPECIFICATION

16H (H = HOME MARKET)

ENGINE Air-cooled vertical single-cylinder, with side valves operated through adjustable tappets. 79mm bore x 100mm stroke = 490cc. Brown & Barlow carburetor with handlebar lever control; CAV magneto ignition.

TRANSMISSION Single-row chain primary and secondary drive, through Sturmey-Archer three-speed transmission with tank-mounted change lever. Ratios 4.5, 7.5, and 12 to 1 for solo use. Kick-start optional.

FRAME Norton-built, lugged and brazed construction.

SUSPENSION Norton Druid front forks; rigid rear frame.

WHEELS Spoked wheels, with 26 x 2.5in (660 x 64mm) Dunlop or Hutchinson tires. Rear brake by block on belt rim; front brake by 5in (127mm) drum.

EQUIPMENT Lyco padded saddle; twin leather toolboxes on rear carrier; tubular rear stand. Lighting set optional.

PERFORMANCE Top speed *c.* 60mph (97km/h).

DIMENSIONS: Wheelbase 54.5in (1384mm), ground clearance 4in (102mm); saddle height 28in (711mm). Fueltank capacity 1.5gal (6l); oil-tank capacity 0.4gal (1.7l).

WEIGHT: 252lb (114kg) dry.

PRICE (1920) £132.

▶ THE 16H WAS DEVELOPED
BY COOPERATION WITH THE
MILITARY AUTHORITIES, AND
HOWARD DRAKE DELEGATED
FROM THE FACTORY TO OVERSEE
MODIFICATIONS THAT WERE
INCORPORATED IN THE
STANDARD SPECIFICATION.

▼ 16Hs IN BULK, AS TROOPS
GO OUT ON A TRAINING RUN IN
PREPARATION FOR MORE
SERIOUS WORK IN WORLD WAR
TWO. PART OF THE TRAINING
SCHEDULE WAS THE ART OF
STEPPING OFF THE MOVING BIKE
IF THE RIDER WAS FIRED UPON.

who had been with the company since 1916,
because a bike came back from road testing with
its exhaust blued from incorrect ignition timing.
From then on, if the inspectors wanted an engine's
timing checked, the very independent "Pop" sent
an innocent apprentice down to deal with the job!

Bikes were chosen at random for road testing, as
fuel was strictly rationed, but all engines were
run-in for 20 minutes on a bench, using the town's
gas supply as fuel. Wartime production reached a
level never seen before, and 100,000 bikes were
built between 1939 and 1945. To manage this, the
factory changed from the system of assembly of a
whole machine by a gang working under a
foreman, to an assembly line. Joe Bates was
recruited from the bigger BSA factory and had
lines of benches built down the length of the
factory floor, with machines built up on wooden
trolleys as they progressed along the line. (The
original benches were still there when the
company moved out 20 years later!)

The 16H, with a modest power output of
12.5bhp to pull a weight of 378 pounds was no
flyer, but its robust build and simple design made

it ideal for the job of teaching novices to ride and maintain. It was used in conditions ranging from desert sands to axle-deep mud and still came back for more punishment.

Sidecar special

The Big 4, used as a sidecar machine, featured sidecar wheel drive to help it through sticky conditions. A simple dog clutch on the special rear wheel drove a shaft to the sidecar wheel and was

engaged by a lever behind the driver's left leg; the dog clutch was protected by a leather gaiter that had to be removed once a week to be repacked with grease. A spare wheel was standard, and the tool kit included a jack to make wheel changing quicker; a Bren gun mounted on the armored sidecar was normal. With three soldiers on board, the Big 4 worked hard to cover ground; and when one came back to the Bracebridge Street factory for serious work, it was regarded as "a major nightmare" by at least one fitter. The sidecar outfit never built up the affectionate following that the solo 16H enjoyed.

The change to overhead valves

When the war in Europe ended, the factory naturally still offered the 16H and Big 4 in its line, but quickly got the more sporting overhead-valve models into production. The side-valve models were old-fashioned, too slow for young men recently released from military service and looking for excitement, and were regarded as really suitable only for pulling sidecars. There was an experimental use of the engine in trials, and factory rider Geoff Duke rode it, but the overhead-valve engine did that job better, too.

1954 was the final year of production life for the 16H and Big 4 side-valve singles. At only £182 6s. (it had retailed at £66 5s. 6d. back in 1916), the 16H was the cheapest model in the line that year, but a claimed 13.5bhp at 4800rpm had little appeal in a world where performance was becoming more important. The Big 4 offered 15.5bhp at 4000rpm for a price of £186, but that, too, was out of its time. By the end of the year, they were both dropped from the line, and a tangible link with James Norton was severed. But they were remembered by many despatch riders for their faithful service during World War Two, and their slogging reliability was valued when they were later sold off for civilian use.

◀ MILITARY BIKES WERE SIMPLE, SO THAT NOVICES COULD EASILY BE TRAINED TO RIDE THEM, AND HANDLEBAR CONTROLS WERE KEPT TO A MINIMUM. THE HEADLIGHT THREW MEAGER LIGHT ONTO THE ROAD AHEAD OF THE FRONT WHEEL, BUT WAS SHROUDED FROM THE VIEW OF ENEMY AIRCRAFT.

◀ THE 16H ENGINE USED THE STANDARD NORTON MEASUREMENTS OF 79MM BORE AND 100MM STROKE; IT WAS TUNED TO RUN ON LOW-GRADE FUELS AND GIVE A MODEST 12.5BHP. THE PRESSED STEEL PRIMARY CHAIN COVER WAS NOT PRETTY, BUT WAS CHEAP TO MAKE AND EASY TO MEND.

▼ THE 633CC BIG FOUR WITH SIDECAR WHEEL DRIVE WAS ADAPTED TO CARRY THREE MEN, ONE MACHINE GUN, AMMUNITION, AND ARMOR PLATING ACROSS COUNTRY.

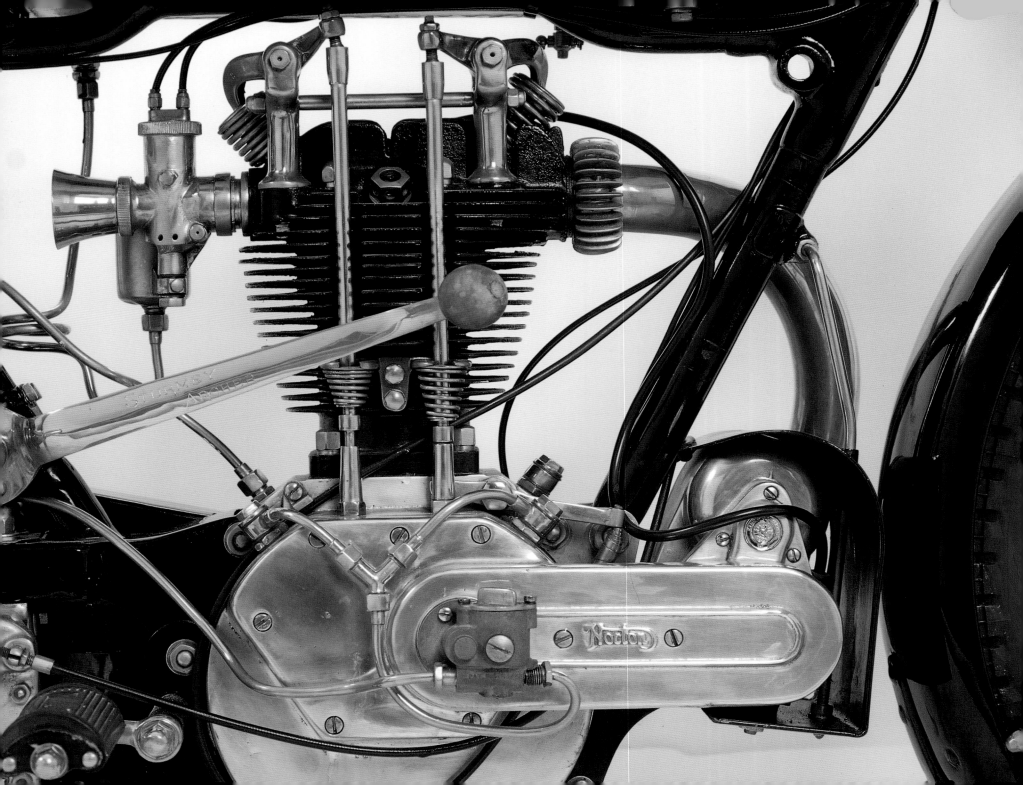

CHAPTER TWO

OVERHEAD VALVES

*O*verhead valves were accepted slowly, but manufacturers with a sporting reputation needed greater power to stay with the more advanced

opposition. In the early 1920s, there were overhead camshaft engines showing the way, as aircraft engine manufacturers looking to fill production lines idle with the end of World War One brought advanced thinking into the market. The pressure was on, and Norton's response was typically thorough but cautious, with a simple pushrod overhead valve conversion to the established engine.

OVERHEAD-VALVE (OHV) engines were regarded with a great deal of suspicion in their early years, when metallurgy was still a young science and valves were unreliable. If a side-valve engine had a valve failure, the damage could be limited, but an overhead valve dropping onto the hard-working piston could prove very expensive. It would certainly be beyond the scope of the roadside repairs that most experienced riders were accustomed to doing; even changing a valve spring would be a major task compared with the ease with which you could perform the same operation on a side valve.

▼ 1922 WAS THE FIRST YEAR OF THE OVERHEAD VALVE NORTON, AND IT NATURALLY FOUND FAVOR WITH SPORTING RIDERS, LIKE I. M. RIDDOCH, A REGULAR COMPETITOR IN SPRINTS.

But by the early 1920s, OHV motors had developed to the point where they performed reliably. In 1921 the Norton factory had the point made very clear to them when five of their faithful side-valves competed in the 500cc Senior TT, and the best they could manage was sixth place. The race was won by Howard Davies on an OHV AJS – and a mere 350cc model at that. The Isle of Man TT races were widely regarded as the most grueling test for sporting road machines, and if an OHV engine could last for six laps of the tough 37.75-mile Mountain Circuit over which the events had been run since 1911, that would convince the man in the street. The move to valves in the cylinder head could not be put off any longer.

The first OHV TT racers

In March 1922 D. R. O'Donovan wheeled out a brand new Norton for his rider, Rex Judd, to have a crack at the 500cc kilometer and mile records; it was their first OHV engine. The engine dimensions were naturally 79mm bore and 100mm stroke, and the wide-set exposed pushrods made it clear that this was the well-proven 16H structure with a different top story. Rex lifted the kilometer record to 89.92mph and the mile to 88.39mph. The overhead-valve Norton had arrived with a real bang.

At the TT – always a race to highlight any mechanical weaknesses – the story was not so good. Ralph Cawthorne started with the new OHV model, but retired on the last lap; the old side-valve models managed fifth and tenth. But at the Ulster Grand Prix later in the season, Hubert Hassall won the 500cc class and was the first man ever to average over 60mph in a road race – on his OHV Norton. The factory was certainly taking the matter of proving their new engine seriously, and had sent competition manager Graham Walker and Hassall to the island ten days before the race to get in plenty of practice.

◀ ULSTERMAN JOE CRAIG
MADE HIS NAME ON A HOME-
TUNED NORTON, WITH FOUR
WINS IN THE ULSTER GRAND
PRIX 600CC CLASS. JOE
LEARNED EARLY THAT TO FINISH
FIRST YOU MUST FIRST FINISH,
AND PREPARED HIS BIKES WITH
RELIABILITY THE MAJOR
REQUIREMENT.

MODEL 18

In 1922 the first overhead-valve Norton was announced. The change in the unit consisted simply of a modern top end being bolted to the well-established bottom end. In the TT that year, the Model 18 failed to finish; but it was fast, and Rex Judd lifted the British 500cc record to 89.9mph (144.74km/h). By 1924 it was a TT winner. The engine in various guises proved to be a versatile unit and continued for over 40 years in the company's line. It performed in every racing discipline and was a sweet and long-legged road engine.

ENGINE Air-cooled vertical single-cylinder, with two overhead valves operated by adjustable pushrods. 79mm bore x 100mm stroke = 490cc. Cast-iron cylinder barrel and head; cast alloy crankcases. Mechanical oil pump.

TRANSMISSION Single-row chain to primary and secondary drive. Dry multi-plate clutch. 3-speed Sturmey-Archer transmission; change lever mounted on right side of fuel tank. Overall gear ratios varied according to buyer's requirements.

FRAME AND SUSPENSION Front Norton-Druid forks at launch, changing to Webb for the 1925 models. Rear frame rigid.

WHEELS Spoked type, with 26 x 2.5in (660 x 64mm) tires. Belt-rim brake at rear, 5in (127mm) drum at front; later models had drum brake at rear.

EQUIPMENT As Model 16H.

PERFORMANCE *c.* 75mph (121km/h) maximum.

DIMENSIONS 54.5in (1384mm) wheelbase; 4in (102mm) ground clearance; 1.5gal (6l) fuel tank; 0.4gal (1.7l) oil tank.

PRICE (1922) £135.

The 490cc Model 18, with three-speed transmission and a drum front brake replacing the old stirrup type used on the 16H, went on display at the Olympia Show later that year, priced at £98. At the 1923 Ulster meeting, there was more success, and the 600cc class went at record speed to Joe Craig, a promising youngster from Ballymena. A man who was to become a central figure in Norton history in the years ahead, Craig won the class for the next three years.

To confirm how fast the new Model 18 was, the factory had arranged for J. D. Pope of the Auto-Cycle Union to visit Bracebridge Street and select the parts from which to build a stock engine. O'Donovan built it into a frame, the bike was shaken down with 29 laps at Brooklands, then locked away in a sealed garage. Next day it was wheeled out, and O'Donovan teamed with Nigel Spring and Bert Denley to break class records from 7 to 12 hours. That year the Maudes Trophy for outstanding achievement with a standard machine had been introduced; Norton's

▼ THE MODEL 18 MAINTAINED THE LONG, LOW BUILD THAT JAMES NORTON CLAIMED WAS THE REASON HIS MACHINES WERE SO STABLE WHEN RIDDEN AT SPEED. THE THREE-SPEED STURMEY-ARCHER TRANSMISSION HAD NO POSITIVE STOP, BUT SKILLED RIDERS COULD CHANGE GEAR QUICKLY.

▶ THE MODEL 18'S ENGINE WAS NATURALLY THE 79MM BORE X 100MM STROKE 490CC NORTON SINGLE CYLINDER MODEL. THE EXPOSED VALVE GEAR NEEDED FREQUENT ATTENTION ON THE LOOSE-SURFACED ROADS OF THE DAY.

demonstration saw the trophy on the boardroom sideboard at Bracebridge Street, and the company went on to win it four years in a row.

Alec Bennett signs on

But for Norton the Senior TT was the ultimate challenge, and in 1924 they signed up Alec Bennett, a freelance Irish-Canadian professional racer, to ride the Model 18 in the Isle of Man. In the Sidecar race, George Tucker of Bristol had a 588cc OHV model with designer and competition manager Walter Moore keeping the third wheel down.

The official record says it all. Bennett, a consummate professional who never won a race at half a mile an hour faster than he needed to, brought the OHV Norton home at a new record average of 61.64mph, the first TT race won at over a mile a minute; second man Harry Langman's Scott was 87 seconds behind. There was quite a contrasting result in the Sidecar race, which Tucker and Moore won by more than half an hour! "Pa" Norton, his health deteriorating fast, was at an official reception given by the Birmingham Corporation when his team returned

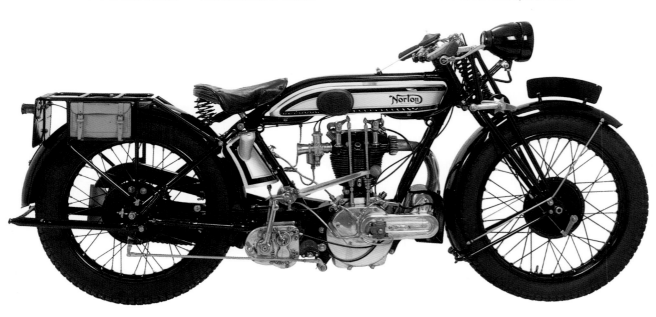

as heroes, but within the year he had succumbed to cancer of the bowel. The industry mourned his passing and subscribed generously to a Norton scholarship in motor engineering at Birmingham University.

There was no victory to celebrate at the 1925 TT, with Alec Bennett third after a fall when he skidded on oil. But in 1926 the great Stanley Woods joined the team and brought home that coveted Senior TT trophy with a new race record speed of 67.54mph. It was to be the last TT victory for the pushrod single, and the overhead-camshaft models took over from then on. However, sidecar drivers Dennis Mansell and Phil Pike continued to use 588cc versions to good effect; in 1926 Pike rode his sidecar outfit up and down the steep and bumpy Bwlch-y-Groes pass in North Wales 100 times, then went on to Edinburgh and Land's End, covering 1531 miles without trouble. The whole epic was closely observed by ACU official Arthur Bourne from the sidecar, and it won the Maudes Trophy for the company for the fourth year. (There is no record of Mr. Bourne getting a medal for his endurance.)

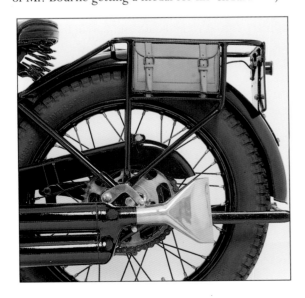

The cradle-frame ES2

In 1928 the ES2 model was added to the line, with a full cradle frame designed by Walter Moore; it was a model name that lived on in various forms until 1963. In 1930 the 350cc JE extended the pushrod engine range. As the OHC models took over the racing side, the pushrod models were promoted as affordable sports models for the discerning, with trials versions available to special order. By 1935 the Model 18 was the second bestseller in the company's line, with the 16H still the cheapest they made and the top seller.

The OHV models dropped out of production soon after Britain declared war on Hitler's Germany in September 1939. But some War Department photos exist, showing a solo ES2 fitted with a sub-machine-gun on a special mounting. How the rider was supposed to control the bike, take aim, and still fire accurately was not made clear!

◀ THE REAR CARRIER WAS A VERSATILE FIXTURE. IT COULD CARRY A WORKMAN'S KNAPSACK, A BUSINESSMAN'S BRIEFCASE, OR EVEN A CUSHION IF A YOUNG LADY COULD BE PERSUADED TO SIT SIDESADDLE AND COME FOR A RIDE.

▲ A CHARACTERISTIC OF THE LATE VINTAGE NORTON WAS THE LEFT-HAND SWEEP OF THE EXHAUST PIPE TO A MUFFLER WITH OPTIONAL FISHTAIL CAP. THE SPRUNG LYCETT SADDLE GAVE A VERY COMFORTABLE RIDE, DESPITE THE RIGID FRAME.

ES2 (EASY-TWO)

In 1927 the ES2 joined the Norton range. The first Norton to be built with a saddle tank, it progressed from cast-iron to alloy cylinder head and from rigid frame to the legendary Featherbed chassis; but it remained the faithful ES2 throughout. The origins of the model title are thought to be E for extra cost, S for sports, and 2 for second version of the OHV

ENGINE Air-cooled vertical single-cylinder, with cast-iron cylinder head and barrel at its launch in 1927. Two overhead valves operated by adjustable pushrods. 79mm bore x 100mm stroke = 490cc. Ignition by magneto mounted behind the cylinder barrel.

TRANSMISSION Single-row chain primary and secondary drive. Dry multi-plate clutch. Sturmey-Archer three-speed transmission, with optional operation either by lever mounted on tank side or by non-positive-stop foot lever.

FRAME AND SUSPENSION Full cradle frame, designed by Walter Moore; lugged and brazed type built in the Frame Shop at Bracebridge Street. Front forks by Webb; rigid rear frame.

WHEELS Spoked. Drum brakes front and rear.

EQUIPMENT Lycett or Dunlop saddle; twin toolboxes on rear carrier; tubular rear stand; lighting and speedometer optional.

▶ THE WAR DEPARTMENT HAD SOME STRANGE IDEAS ABOUT THE BEST WAY TO RESIST INVASION. HOW THE RIDER WAS TO KEEP CONTROL, TAKE AIM, AND FIRE ACCURATELY IS NOT CLEAR. THE DOUBLE-BARRELED MUFFLER WAS FITTED FOR 1938 AND KNOWN IN THE FACTORY AS "THE COW'S UDDER."

THE 1932 ES2 WAS A SPORTS MODEL WITH FULL CRADLE FRAME, LARGE BRAKES, AND A TOP SPEED APPROACHING 80MPH.

Telescopic forks

Peace came to Europe in 1945, and the Norton factory switched production from military to civilian models, with the Model 18 and the ES2 back on offer to a transportation-hungry world. The obvious difference was the fitting of "Roadholder" telescopic forks in the 1946 season, developed from the more basic types fitted to the 1938 racing machines. For trials work, a batch of six Model 18s was built and sent out to selected riders. One of the six is known to survive. It was found in a field with a sidecar welded to it before the long process of restoration began. All these bikes had rigid rear frames and telescopic forks, but the plunger-sprung rear end was added to the list of options for the road-going models in 1946.

Geoff Duke arrives

One-day trials were important show-places for leading makers, and Norton recruited talent to take on rivals like AJS, BSA, and Royal Enfield. Rex Young from Middlesbrough was one of the best, and in 1948 he was joined by a young man

◄ GEOFF DUKE WAS INVOLVED
IN THE DEVELOPMENT OF THE
500T TRIALS MODEL AND RODE
IT FOR THE FACTORY WHEN
ROAD RACING ALLOWED. HERE
HE IS IN THE 1952 BEMROSE
TRIAL IN DERBYSHIRE, FINDING
A WAY THROUGH THE STREAM
BUT NOT INTO THE AWARDS.

▼ AN UNDATED PICTURE FROM
THE FACTORY'S OWN
EXPERIMENTAL DEPARTMENT. A
500T BUILT TO AN UNUSUAL
SPECIFICATION, WITH ROAD
TIRES, AN AMAL TT
CARBURETOR AND FULL
LIGHTING SET. ITS DESTINY IS A
MYSTERY.

fresh from military service, Geoff Duke, to work in the grandly named Experimental Shop. "In truth it was about 10 feet square and terribly cramped," is the way Geoff remembers the shop in those early days. His arrival at Bracebridge Street coincided with the development of the 500T trials model, its 79mm x 100mm (what else, from Norton?) engine in a special frame with a 53-inch wheelbase, ground clearance of 7in and a weight of 300 pounds.

The 500T was a success for the factory, with Geoff Duke winning the important Victory Trial at Church Stretton in Shropshire, England, in early

1950 before moving on to develop his road-racing career. Bob Woolaway won the Kickham Trial, in Wiltshire, and the elegant style of the tall Rex Young took his 500T to wins in the Travers, Pennines, the Allan Jeffries in Yorkshire, and the Manville events in Warwickshire. At the end of the season, the best Norton in the British Experts Trial in Church Stretton, Shropshire, was young Duke in fifth place, just to prove that he hadn't lost his touch.

For 1951 the teenaged Jeff Smith joined Bob Clayton and Rex Young in the team and won the Lomax Trial in North Wales, and the Traders Cup

Trial in Shropshire to confirm his promise; but Rex Young rode consistently throughout the season to finish second in the ACU Trials Drivers' Star, the national championship in everything but name. John Draper was third in the 1953 ACU Star battle; but it was clear that Norton were slipping out of contention and at the end of that season Draper, Smith, and Young all switched to BSA. The 500T was out of the line by the start of the 1955 season, but it lived on as a competitive sidecar machine in the hands of drivers like Peter Roydhouse.

▼ THE 1957 MODEL 19S WAS SOMETHING OF AN ENIGMA, WITH ITS SLOGGING 600CC ENGINE THAT THE PUBLIC HAD ONCE WANTED TO PULL A SIDECAR, AND DRESSED IN SPORTING STYLE IN A SPRING FRAME MADE IN NORTON'S OWN FRAME SHOP. IT DID NOT LAST LONG IN THE LINE.

▼ THE 500T HAS KEPT ITS REPUTATION AMONG TRIALS MEN, AND WITH THE GROWING POPULARITY OF PRE-65 EVENTS IT IS IN ACTION AGAIN. THIS IS CLIVE DOPSON ON HIS FINE 1949 EXAMPLE, ENJOYING HIMSELF IN THE 1994 PRE-65 SCOTTISH TRIAL.

London meant the end for the 79mm x 100mm ES2 and its echoes of that fine old man, James Lansdowne Norton.

In recent years pushrod singles have had a revival in historic racing, where their lower price has made them an affordable alternative to the noble Manx. In 1986 Colin Dally won the Vintage Club's 500cc championship against opposition with far better racing pedigrees. A maintenance fitter at an aircraft factory, Dally produces his own steel crankshaft with an 88mm stroke, and on the Jawa speedway conrod he fits an 84mm piston from a BSA Gold Star. He also makes his own valves and camshafts, while the plain big-end bearings are simply the camshaft bearings from a Ford car engine. The result is a machine that looks like an innocent ES2, but revs to 7000 and has been measured giving 42bhp at the back wheel, running on gasoline.

This way of confounding prejudice against the pushrod Norton extends to Dally's Model 50, which won the Vintage Club's 350 title in 1987, beating BSA Gold Star opposition. "The pushrod Norton is probably the most simple engine there is," claims Dally. "And it's really reliable – I've never had anything break."

Swinging-arm frame

The roadster's plunger-sprung frame was replaced by a swinging-arm version in 1953, but the pushrod road models were still available only as 500s – the faithful old ES2 and Model 18. By 1955 the 596cc Model 19 was added, with swinging-arm rear end for the solo riders and a rigid one for conservative sidecar drivers. But the developments in the small-car world, with inexpensive models like the Morris Minor, Austin A30, and Standard 8, were a real threat to the sidecar combination as traditional family transportation, and the rigid Model 19's aim to be a replacement for the obsolete Big 4 side-valve never proved realistic. Mr. and Mrs. Everybody now wanted a steel body and windshield around them when it rained.

Sluggish but safe

In 1959 came the final development of the OHV roadsters, with the Models 18 and 19 dropped and the ES2 motor fitted into the Featherbed frame that had given the company's image such a lift. It was joined by the 350cc Model 50, once described to me by an experienced old hand as "the safest motorcycle in the world – the best frame, the best brakes and the slowest engine."

It was an opinion based on fact. The standard Model 50 would struggle to get above 65mph with a pillion passenger on the comfortable dual seat, while the bigger muscles of the ES2's engine made a steady 75mph feel easy. But in 1963 the move of the Norton factory from its traditional Bracebridge Street home to join AJS and Matchless in east

◀ THE NATIONAL
MOTORCYCLE MUSEUM, AT
BICKENHILL NEAR BIRMINGHAM,
ENGLAND, HAS THIS
BEAUTIFULLY RESTORED 1952

500T AND CONTEMPORARY
WATSONIAN TRAILS SIDECAR.
NONE OF THEM STAYED IN THIS
SPOTLESS CONDITION FOR
LONG!

1952/3 ES2 500 SINGLE

The ES2 was one of the longest lasting of Norton's models, spanning the years from the spindly rigid-framed models of the 1920s through to the Featherbed-framed version of the 1960s. Its appeal as a sturdy, simple workhorse with spirit endured throughout that time and it is still highly prized by both collectors and serious riders. It served with the Royal Automobile Club, hauling large box sidecars of tools and equipment as patrolmen went to the aid of drivers. It was never a glamorous machine, and it was always near the bottom of the company's price range; but it won countless friends over the years. The specification below is for the 1953 version.

ENGINE Air-cooled vertical single-cylinder, with two valves operated by pushrods; ignition by magneto; carburation by Amal. 79mm bore x 100mm stroke = 490cc. Compression ratio 6.2:1. Dry-sump lubrication by rotary pump.

TRANSMISSION Primary and final drive by single-row chain, via dry multi-plate clutch in oil-bath primary chaincase. Four-speed Norton transmission with foot operation, standard solo ratios 14.2, 8.5, 5.75 and 4.75 to 1.

FRAME AND SUSPENSION Norton-built lugged and brazed cradle frame with single top tube. Suspension by Norton Roadholder telescopic forks with swinging-arm at rear.

WHEELS Spoked, with 19 x 3.25in (483 x 83mm) front and 19 x 3.5in (483 x 89mm) rear tires. Half-width drum brakes, 7in (178mm) diameter front and rear.

EQUIPMENT Lycett cushion saddle; pillion and pillion footrests optional. Lighting by Lucas; speedometer by Smith's.

PERFORMANCE Maximum speed *c.* 80mph (129km/h).

DIMENSIONS Wheelbase 54.5in (1384mm), ground clearance 6.5in (165mm), saddle height 31in (787mm), weight 396lb (167kg).

POWER 25bhp at 5300rpm.

PRICE £209 11s.

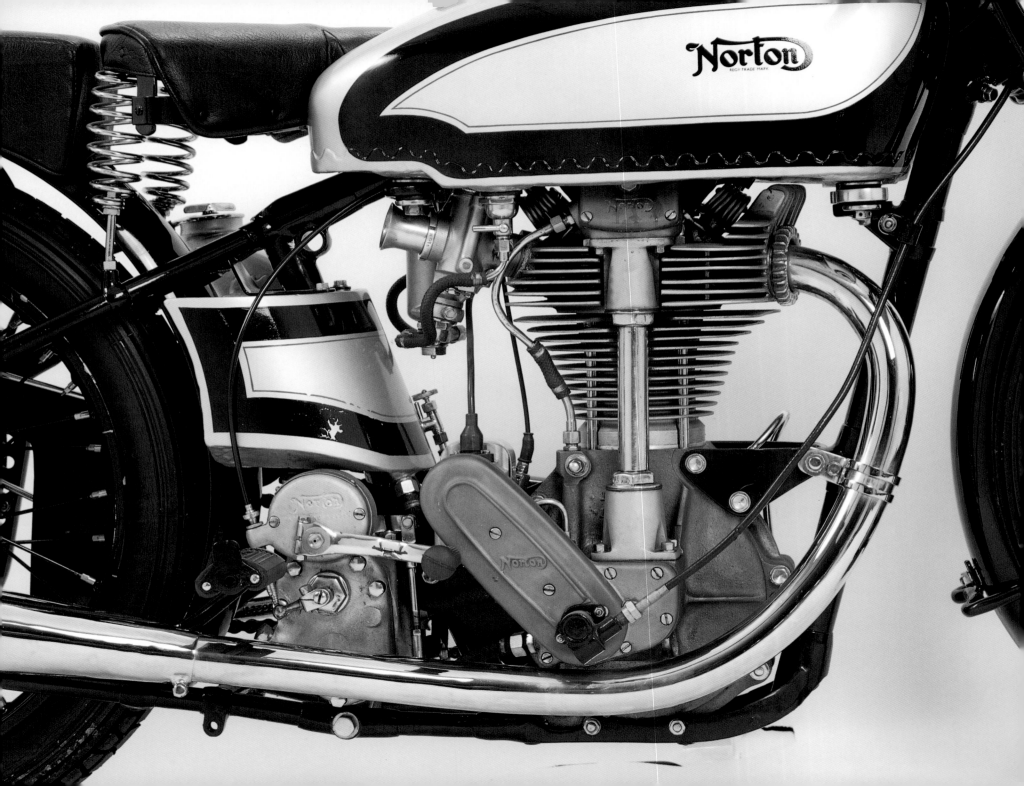

CHAPTER THREE

OVERHEAD CAMSHAFTS

*I*n the mid-1920s, racing success was becoming
an essential part of presenting Norton's speed,
handling, and reliability to the world; a win in the
Isle of Man TT races proved all three.
They were on the treadmill of success
and needed to meet the opposition
coming from Velocette's overhead
camshaft motor and Rudge's four-valver. The
answer came from Walter Moore's drawing board,
with a single overhead cam driven from the
crankshaft via a vertical shaft and bevel gears.

IN THE YEARS between the two world wars, Norton had a reputation far bigger than the size of its Bracebridge Street factory really justified, a name built on speed and sporting success. The Isle of Man TT wins in 1924 and 1926 brought wide publicity because those races were regarded all over the world as the greatest test of man and machine. It consisted, from 1926, of seven laps of the Mountain Circuit – 264.25 miles over closed public highways including the long climb up Snaefell (2034ft). Once the company had established its habit of success and the publicity it brought, it recognized the need to keep ahead of the opposition. Naturally, their rivals weren't planning to give up the fight, and there were signs of a new type of engine offering a serious threat: overhead-camshaft units.

In 1925 the world-record one-kilometer speed for the 350cc class was lifted above 100mph (161km/h) by Dougal Marchant on a Chater Lea with a Blackburne overhead-camshaft engine; no 500cc Norton had officially topped the magic "ton" at that time. That same year Alec Bennett rode the new overhead-camshaft Velocette in the 350cc Junior TT and won easily. It was clear that the future, at least in terms of high-performance bikes, lay with overhead camshafts – so Norton got on with the job of designing one. The result was an engine that powered the great-grandfather of one of the all-time classic racing bikes.

The CS1 and CJ1

Walter Moore was the man at Bracebridge Street in charge of competition, and he came up with a tall, elegant motor with Norton's traditional 79mm bore and 100mm stroke. The single overhead camshaft was driven by bevel gears on a vertical shaft from the crankshaft on the right side of the motor, and it opened the valves via short, exposed rockers. CS1 was its title (for Camshaft Senior One) and in 1928 it was joined by the 71mm x 88mm 350cc CJ1 (Camshaft Junior One). The CS1 was for Norton's Senior TT contenders, the CJ1 for the Junior TT: as always the Isle of Man dominated Norton's sporting activities.

Stanley Woods showed how fast the CS1 was by carving out a lead of no less than four minutes in the 1927 Senior TT. Unfortunately he was given no signals by his pit staff to indicate the extent of his lead, and he pressed on until his clutch gave up. Alec Bennett on another CS1 had been pacing himself and moved up to claim another victory, the first man to win three TT races. No matter that the new Norton design was said to be similar to that of the Velocette and Blackburne OHC engines: it was a winner. After the TT, Stanley Woods confirmed it with wins in the 500cc Belgian and Swiss Grands Prix as well as the Dutch TT.

Arthur Carroll's 1930 engine

The CS1 failed to hold its advantage over the opposition in 1928, and there were few successes until a shake-up saw Moore leave to join NSU in Germany (at a rumored £5,000 a year and a company house with servants – very different from the modest rewards at Norton), and Joe Craig was brought in as competition manager from 1929. A star rider in his own right, Craig was a tactician supreme. By 1930 he had a new engine, partly the product of his own experience, but owing most to the design flair of the shy Arthur Carroll. It would be difficult to overstate the dominance that this engine exercised in racing in years to come: born in 1930, its basic layout is still seen in Manx Norton engines built today.

The new model took a few months to bring to race-winning trim, and Norton was soundly

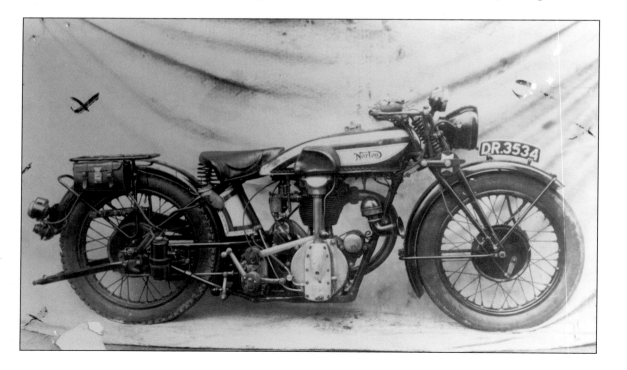

◀ EVEN IN ITS 350CC CJ1 FORM, WALTER MOORE'S OVERHEAD CAMSHAFT ENGINE STOOD PROUD AND TALL, WHICH RATHER LIMITED ITS GROUND CLEARANCE. THE RIDER OF THIS BIKE HAS PROBABLY EXPERIENCED SOME NEARSIGHTED MOTORISTS, TO JUDGE FROM THE ELECTRIC KLAXON.

▼ MOORE'S MODEL WAS DROPPED IN FAVOR OF THE ARTHUR CARROLL DESIGN WHEN IT FAILED TO KEEP UP ITS RACE-WINNING FORM. MOORE JOINED NSU IN GERMANY AND DREW UP A CLOSE RELATION OF THE CS1, CLAIMING THAT HE DESIGNED THE ORIGINAL IN HIS OWN TIME AND IT WAS HIS PROPERTY.

CS1 (CAMSHAFT SENIOR ONE)

Walter Moore's elegant overhead-camshaft engine was introduced in 1927 and showed its speed with a Senior TT win in the hands of Alec Bennett. Its production life was brief after a redesign of the cylinder head produced less power; it was replaced by the Arthur Carroll design that, developed over 30 years, evolved into the definitive single-cylinder racer. The CS1 was available as a sports machine in 1929 and set a fashion for road-going bikes with a clear relationship to the machines that raced so successfully in Norton's colors.

ENGINE Air-cooled vertical single-cylinder; two valves operated by rockers from single overhead camshaft driven from crankshaft by vertical shaft and bevel gears. 79mm bore x 100 stroke = 490cc. Amal carburetor; Lucas magneto ignition; dry-sump lubrication with separate oil tank. Estimated power 30bhp at 6000rpm.

TRANSMISSION Single-row chain primary and secondary drive; primary, in cast aluminum case, via dry multi-plate clutch. Three-speed Sturmey-Archer transmission with positive-stop foot change. Standard road ratios 4.42, 5.87, and 10.6 to 1; alternative close ratios 4.42, 5.87, and 7.8 to 1.

FRAME AND SUSPENSION Norton-built full cradle frame of lugged and brazed construction, with single top tube. Webb girder front forks; rigid rear frame.

WHEELS Spoked, 26 x 3.25in (660 x 83mm) tires, 7in (178mm) drum front brake, 8in (203mm) rear.

EQUIPMENT Dunlop rubber seat; twin leather toolboxes attached to rear carrier; Lucas lighting set optional.

PERFORMANCE Maximum speed c. 90mph (145km/h).

DIMENSIONS 54.5in (1384mm) wheelbase, 4.25in (108mm) ground clearance, 3.6gal (13.6l) alloy saddle-type fuel tank; 1.2gal (4.6l) oil tank.

SPECIFICATION

▼ BY 1934 THE CS1 WAS CATALOGUED AS THE INTERNATIONAL AND A RENOWNED SPORTS MACHINE. *Motor Cycling* MAGAZINE TESTED ONE AND FACTORY RACER JIMMY SIMPSON RECORDED A TOP SPEED OF 100MPH, REMARKABLE FOR A ROAD-EQUIPPED 500.

MODEL 30 INTERNATIONAL

The Arthur Carroll designed overhead-camshaft engine was first made available to the buying public in 1931 and set the pattern for one of the great sporting road machines of the 1930s. Its close physical relationship to the bikes ridden by the most successful team in racing was a great sales aid. When one magazine wanted a rider to check its top speed, factory rider Jimmy Simpson obliged and recorded 100mph (161km/h) on a public road; an astonishing speed for a road-equipped 500cc machine. The Model 30 continued in production until 1956, its engine virtually unchanged; by then it was left behind on performance by BSA's very well developed Gold Star.

ENGINE Air-cooled vertical single-cylinder; two valves controlled by hairpin springs operated by rockers from single camshaft driven by vertical shaft and bevel gears top and bottom. 79mm bore x 100mm stroke = 490cc. Alloy cylinder head with bronze skull; iron barrel with alloy option available.

TRANSMISSION Three-speed Sturmey-Archer transmission at introduction in 1931; later, four-speed Norton with overall ratios of 4.64, 5.1, 6.16, and 10.8 to 1; foot change. Single-row chain primary and secondary drive.

FRAME Cradle lugged and brazed assembly at introduction, with plunger rear suspension as an option from 1938 at an extra cost of £7 10s. Webb girder forks until 1946, when Roadholder telescopic forks fitted. Featherbed frame with Roadholder forks and swinging-arm rear suspension from 1954.

WHEELS Spoked 21in (533mm) front and 20in (508mm) rear; from 1954, 19in (483mm) front and rear. Dunlop tires; 7in (178mm) drum single leading-shoe front brake; 8in (203mm) rear.

EQUIPMENT Speedometer and Lucas lighting optional at introduction; standard from mid 1930s. Horn and licence holder standard in 1938.

PERFORMANCE Maximum speed *c.* 100mph (161km/h) in 1932; *c.* 110mph (177km/h) in 1954.

DIMENSIONS (1955 Featherbed) 4.2gal (16l) tank; 55.5in (1410mm) wheelbase, 6.75in (172mm) ground clearance, 31in (787mm) saddle height.

WEIGHT (1955): 380lb (173kg).

POWER *c.* 29bhp at 6200rpm.

PRICE (1931) £72; (1938) £102 11s.; (1955) £273.12s.

beaten by the four-valve Rudges at the TT. But by the end of its first season, the Carroll engine had carried Stanley Woods to victory in the Ulster Grand Prix and Jimmy Simpson to a win in the Swedish Grand Prix. It was clearly a very sound motor, and at the end of 1930 the factory announced that it would be available in its 350 and 500 road machines. This series was given the official title of "International." But when a customer ordered one in full competition trim to ride in the Manx Grand Prix, the work sheet attached to it at the factory was stamped "Manx."

▼TIM HUNT WAS THE FIRST RIDER TO WIN THE 350CC JUNIOR AND 500CC SENIOR TTS IN ONE WEEK. RECRUITED TO THE TEAM AFTER SUCCESS IN THE MANX GRAND PRIX, HE MADE HIS WINS IN 1931, TO MARK THE BEGINNING OF NORTON'S PERIOD OF COMPLETE DOMINATION OF INTERNATIONAL RACING.

This was the name used on the factory floor, and it later passed into legend.

Glory days with Woods and Guthrie

From 1931 the Norton team made international racing its own, with Joe Craig recruiting the best talent available and giving them the bikes to win on. The experienced Stanley Woods was teamed with rising star Tim Hunt, with Scotsman Jimmy Guthrie in support. Hunt won the 350 and 500 TTs in 1931, Woods did the same in 1932 and 1933, and Guthrie did it again in 1934. It was total domination – the most important races in the international calendar captured by one team, even when its stars moved on or retired, as Hunt was forced to do after a crash in the 1933 Swedish Grand Prix left him with a badly damaged leg.

Stanley Woods signed on with the Swedish Husqvarna team in 1934 (he had his first ride on the 500cc V-twin in a local ice race when he visited the factory), so Jimmy Guthrie took over from Tim Hunt as team leader and proved to be a superstar.

Guthrie was an extremely fit little Scot, partner with his brother in a garage business in the Borders town of Hawick. Every spring a Norton would be delivered to the garage, and Jimmy would get in practice with some rapid outings on the road alongside the London to Edinburgh rail route. The crews got to know the lone rider of a silver and black Norton who could cover ground on those lightly trafficked roads faster than their express train.

▲ ON THE VERY WET SOUTHPORT SANDS ON THE NORTHWESTERN COAST OF ENGLAND IN OCTOBER 1932, HARRY LEVINGS HAD A VERY SUCCESSFUL DAY ON HIS 350 INTERNATIONAL. HE WON THE 11-MILE AND 25-MILE RACES, AND WENT FAST ENOUGH TO FINISH SECOND IN THE 750CC CLASS IN THE LONGER RACE.

Frith joins the team

Freddie Frith, a tough young stonemason from Lincolnshire was drafted into the team in 1936, to join Guthrie and Cambridge graduate John "Crasher" White. Frith went straight into Joe Craig's good books in the 1936 Junior TT, when team leader Guthrie was delayed with mechanical problems and the new man got frantic signals to speed up. He responded with a new class lap record at 81.94mph and won a TT on his first ride. That left no doubt about his team place being secure.

Fifty years later, Frith could still clearly recall the German Grand Prix of that year. "We had to travel to Germany by train," he explained. "We were just told to report at the Nurburgring for practice and were expected to find our own way. The mechanics were already there with the bikes; the team had rented a farmhouse and the washhouse was the workshop." Matched against the might of Germany's DKW, BMW, and NSU teams, backed by the state as Hitler put the Third Reich's sporting and technical expertise on show, the Norton team's effort seemed modest compared with the special transporters and spare machines of the home teams. But Guthrie won the 500 and new boy Frith the 350: "I was almost overwhelmed, winning against all that lot and standing up there on the rostrum as they played our national anthem," he remembered with a quiet smile.

▼ THE 1936 INTERNATIONAL CAME WITH A RIGID FRAME AND NO OPTIONS. BUT THE RACING TEAM WERE SOON TO SHOW HOW EFFECTIVE SPRING FRAMES COULD BE FOR SPEED WORK, AND THE FACTORY OFFERED THEM ON SPECIAL ORDER ONCE THE DESIGN WAS PROVED IN COMPETITION.

The Guthrie tragedy

At the 1937 Swiss Grand Prix, Guthrie won the 500 and did it again in Belgium. Then came a tragedy that rocked the motorcycling world. The German Grand Prix, another clash of Norton determination and German might, was next on the calendar. Guthrie was leading the 500, looking an easy winner, when he crashed on the last lap; he died of his injuries that night. He was the supreme rider of his day and was a hero to many thousands. The Norton team did not race again that year.

Freddie Frith remembered Guthrie with affection and respect: "A real gentleman. He was very helpful and I learned a lot from him in my early days with Norton." To this day, his memorial

◀ FREDDIE FRITH HAD A STYLE THAT SUGGESTED SPEED, AND HIS PERFORMANCE LIVED UP TO IT. IN THE 1937 SENIOR TT, HE BEAT STANLEY WOODS' VELOCETTE WITH A NEW RACE RECORD AND LIFTED THE LAP RECORD OVER 90MPH FOR THE FIRST TIME AT 90.27MPH.

▼ FRITH SWEEPING WIDE ON THE EXIT FROM CREG-NY-BAA AND AVOIDING THE THREATENING STONE WALLS THAT LINE MUCH OF THE TT COURSE. HE WAS ONE OF THE FIRST PROFESSIONAL RACERS TO FOLLOW A FITNESS PROGRAM AND MANAGED TO FINISH GRUELING RACES LIKE THESE LOOKING FRESH.

Plunger suspension

In 1936 the factory racers were fitted with plunger rear suspension, and Frith certainly liked it: "Made the bikes much more comfortable to ride in a long race like the TT." Guthrie's record bears that out, with the 500cc Senior TT and the 500 Belgian, Dutch, German, and Swiss Grands Prix all falling to him that year. Then in 1937 Guthrie won the 350 TT and Frith the 500, Frith putting in the first ever 90mph lap of the TT circuit after Guthrie had retired. It was a feat of skill and strength typical of the stars of the day, who had to compete on what were largely country roads on bikes with very limited suspension travel, only four speeds in the transmission, and tires that lacked the grip taken for granted today. These limiting factors forced riders to master techniques that demanded just as much skill and subtlety as those employed today. As Frith remarked many years later: "They talk about cadence braking today, but we used to do the same thing. If it was wet, you'd give the brake a bit of a nidge to take the speed down a little bit." Action pictures of the time suggest a very physical high-speed wrestling match, but the approach was much more refined.

◀ CRYSTAL PALACE IN
LONDON HOSTED THE
SYDENHAM VASE RACES IN
1938, AND LOCAL STAR JACK
SURTEES WAS UNBEATABLE IN
THE SIDECAR RACES, EVEN IF HIS
PASSENGER DID TRY TO WEAR
THE ASPHALT OUT. IN THE
1950S JACK'S SON JOHN WAS A
RISING STAR.

statue in Hawick regularly has fresh flowers at its base; and there is another memorial to him a few miles south of Ramsey on the Isle of Man Mountain Circuit, scene of so many of his triumphs.

Daniell's record lap

For 1938 Frith was team leader, riding with the first telescopic forks the factory had made, sprung but not damped; Londoner Harold Daniell was drafted in to join him and "Crasher" White. Daniell made history with a record-breaking 91mph lap to snatch the Senior TT on the final lap, after a race-long battle with Frith and Stanley Woods (Velocette); that record would remain unbeaten until 1950. In the 350cc TT, Woods and Ted Mellors on the new swinging-arm Velocettes beat Frith to end Norton's run of seven wins in a row.

In the 500cc class foreign machines – notably the supercharged BMW twin and Gilera's four-cylinder were showing the way in the European

GPs, and George Meier on his BMW won five of the 500 races. Frith came second in the Belgian, the enamel on the front forks shotblasted off by the gravel thrown up by the BMW'S rear wheel as Frith desperately slipstreamed the faster bike. Daniell won the 350 and 500 Swiss races, with Frith close behind. But at the end of the year, Norton's factory team withdrew from racing, and the company concentrated on the production of humble 16H side-valve models for the Army. The racers were made available on loan to the team members for the 1939 season.

Frith rode his heart out in the 500 TT, but Georg Meier and Jock West on BMWs were just too fast for him. At the Ulster Grand Prix, he led for half the race; then Dario Serafini on the supercharged four-cylinder Gilera took over. It was a devastating show of the Italian machine's speed. When he wrote of the race in Geoff Davison's Racing Reminiscences, Frith recalled going flat out at 120mph: "I wasn't surprised to see Serafini draw alongside, but I was rather

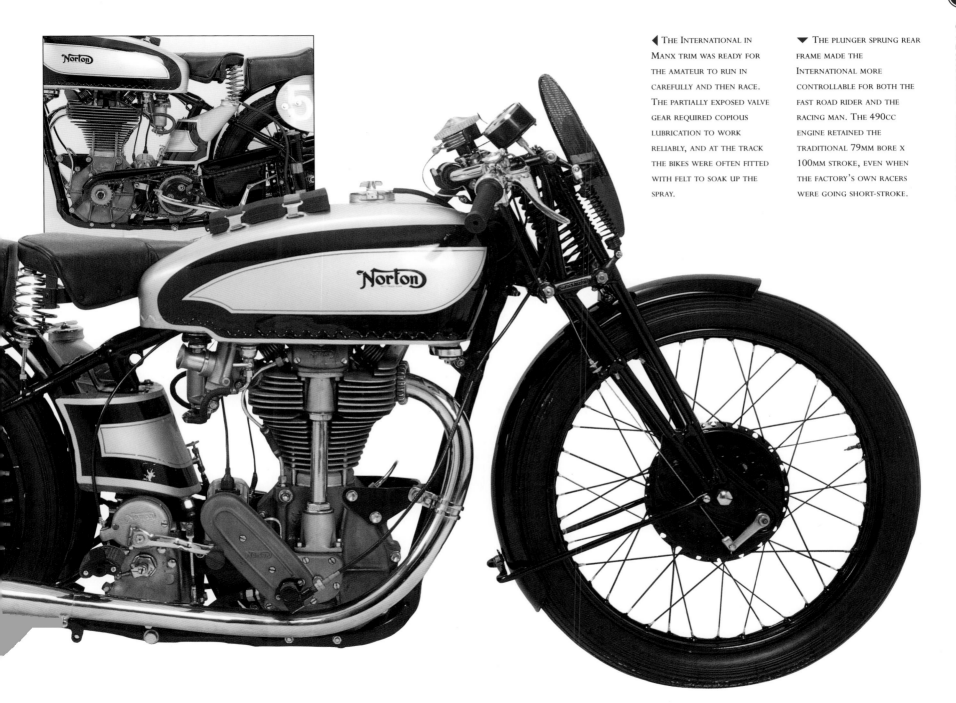

◀ THE INTERNATIONAL IN
MANX TRIM WAS READY FOR
THE AMATEUR TO RUN IN
CAREFULLY AND THEN RACE.
THE PARTIALLY EXPOSED VALVE
GEAR REQUIRED COPIOUS
LUBRICATION TO WORK
RELIABLY, AND AT THE TRACK
THE BIKES WERE OFTEN FITTED
WITH FELT TO SOAK UP THE
SPRAY.

▼ THE PLUNGER SPRUNG REAR
FRAME MADE THE
INTERNATIONAL MORE
CONTROLLABLE FOR BOTH THE
FAST ROAD RIDER AND THE
RACING MAN. THE 490CC
ENGINE RETAINED THE
TRADITIONAL 79MM BORE X
100MM STROKE, EVEN WHEN
THE FACTORY'S OWN RACERS
WERE GOING SHORT-STROKE.

▼ A 1947 500 CC MANX, REBUILT TO ORIGINAL SPECIFICATION BY JOURNALIST JOHN GRIFFITH AFTER A LONG SEARCH FOR CORRECT PARTS. THE BALL-ENDED CONTROL LEVERS ARE A LATER REQUIREMENT, FITTED TO MAKE THE MACHINE LEGAL FOR RACING.

▶ UNIDENTIFIED RIDER, WASTING NO TIME AT SIGNPOST CORNER IN THE PRACTICE FOR THE 1948 MANX GRAND PRIX. THE MANX NORTON WAS THE UNCHALLENGED CHOICE FOR THE PRIVATE OWNER IN THE 500CC CLASS, BUT IN TWO YEARS' TIME, THE FEATHERBED FRAME WAS TO MAKE IT OUTDATED.

staggered to see him sitting almost upright and taking his ease. What really shook me . . . was to see him give a friendly grin, take a large handful of grip, and disappear into the blue."

Post-war revival

The writing was clearly on the wall for the aging single-cylinder Norton, but Adolf Hitler had greater ambitions than finally putting the old British warrior to sleep. He kickstarted the war in Europe, and racing there came to an end for seven years. It started up again in 1946, but it was 1947

before international events were organized.

In Britain there was a new class of races catering for club members entered on standard production models; its first outstanding contribution to the racing scene was providing Geoff Duke with the opportunity to clinch his first Isle of Man victory in the 1949 races. The early years of the Clubman's TT were Norton-dominated, but Harold Clark on a BSA Gold Star won the 1948 350cc race and hinted at developments to come from the pushrod engine that finally eclipsed Norton's International.

Ulstermen Artie Bell and Ernie Lyons and 1938 Manx Grand Prix winner Ken Bills were recruited into the factory team to join Harold Daniell for the 1947 season. Norton had approached Freddie Frith, but he declined: "I didn't get on with [CEO] Gilbert Smith. He could be a bit sneaky," was his terse explanation years later. The riders had prewar bikes, rescued from their secret wartime storage, updated with better front forks and detuned to run on the poor-quality "pool" fuel then available.

During the war, Harold Daniell had been turned down for military service because his eyesight was too bad, but at the TT it was good enough for him to see the way to another 500cc Senior win. Newcomer Bell was 22 seconds behind at the flag, to reward all the time he put into learning the sequence of bends on the formidable course; he would spend evenings in his hotel room reeling them off while his wife checked his memory against a course plan. Bell was to win the Senior TT in 1948, after a titanic battle with Daniell, and the two men dominated international 500cc racing in the immediately post-war years.

The World Championships

For 1949 there was a new challenge: the first World Championships. It was not a convenient time for Norton; Joe Craig, the team's guiding light, had temporarily withdrawn from the active

racing scene to concentrate on the development of a four-cylinder engine in collaboration with Raymond Mays' ERA (English Racing Automobile) company. In Craig's absence, the factory retained tuner Steve Lancefield to run the Norton Racing Syndicate. Lancefield was a partner with his brother-in-law Harold Daniell in a south London dealership. At Norton he had a tight budget; a talented team of Bell, Daniell, and newcomer Johnny Lockett — and very little else. Even spares as basic as piston rings were limited. Daniell won the 1949 Senior TT, but that was the team's only world-championship race win that year. Les Graham on the AJS won the very first 500cc world title, while Freddie Frith on his Velocette dominated the 350cc class completely — and then announced his retirement from the sport. Norton had one championship to its credit with Eric Oliver winning the first of his four world sidecar

◀ HAROLD DANIELL WON HIS THIRD SENIOR TT IN 1949, BUT LEFT HIS OWN 91MPH LAP RECORD FROM 1938 INTACT.

▲ ERIC OLIVER (ABOVE AND TOP) WAS A GOOD SOLO RIDER, CAPABLE OF WINNING RACES IN GOOD COMPANY. AS A SIDECAR DRIVER, HE STOOD HEAD AND SHOULDERS ABOVE THE REST.

titles with a unique twin-cam version of the 596cc sidecar racing motor. Norton's chief executive Gilbert Smith consoled Steve Lancefield with the remark: "Never mind. You got the one that counts most of all – the Senior TT."

At the end of 1949 there was no doubt that the Norton racers, still closely based on the late-1930s models, could not hope to beat potent new machines like the AJS "Porcupine" twin and Gilera's four-cylinder model as they developed. The Manx model might be an obvious choice for the ambitious private owner, but, in the headline-making Grands Prix that helped to sell ordinary road machines, they needed something better.

Strength in depth

The 500cc Manx Norton's strength in depth was as the bike for an ambitious racer in the premier class; it was rivaled only by Triumph's fast but fragile Grand Prix – a bike that evoked the comment from Northampton racer Joe Glazebrook's mechanic: "They ought to fit a wire cage around the motor to catch the bits when it blows up!"

The Norton just kept on winning. At the Daytona Beach Race, Ohio farmer Dick Klamfoth and Canadian Bill Matthews conquered the challenge of a mixed sand and asphalt course. In South Africa their champion was the fiery Borro Castellani, dominating the long-distance handicap races on a variety of tracks that included the Jimmy Guthrie circuit at Jameson Park.

In Australia and New Zealand, future stars like Harry Hinton, George Morrison, and Ken Mudford learned their racing on the plunger-sprung Manx with its 79mm bore x 100mm stroke 490cc engine that dated back to Arthur Carroll's design of the late 1920s. It was a versatile engine, used by Norton team members in the International Six Days Trial in 1948 and by the Humphries brothers in their very successful one-day trials

▲ THE 596CC OVERHEAD CAMSHAFT ENGINES BUILT IN THE 1930S FOR SIDECAR RACING WERE STILL COMPETITIVE IN THE 1950S. DON SLATE, WHOSE OUTFIT WAS FAST BUT NOT LIKELY TO WIN A BEAUTY CONTEST, USED HIS FOR ROAD AND GRASS TRACK RACING.

▼ THE FACTORY ENTERED
THREE SPECIALLY BUILT
INTERNATIONALS IN THE 1948
INTERNATIONAL SIX DAYS
TRIAL, BUT WITH NO NUMBERS
IT IS NOT POSSIBLE TO IDENTIFY
WHOSE MOUNT THIS WAS.
ROAD TIRES WERE FOR TESTING
PURPOSES AND RUNNING-IN.

careers. Les Archer, from the famous Aldershot racing family, developed a scramble version, and in 1956 he won the very first European Moto Cross Championship.

The plain fact was that, for road racing at the highest level, Norton was lagging behind in both engine and chassis development. In the latter department, however, better things were on the way.

▲ LES ARCHER, ONE OF THE FAMOUS RACING FAMILY FROM ALDERSHOT (HAMPSHIRE) WON THE 1956 EUROPEAN MOTO CROSS CHAMPIONSHIP ON AN OVERHEAD CAMSHAFT NORTON IN A SPECIAL FRAME. HERE HE IS ON HOME SOIL, AT HAWKSTONE PARK IN ENGLAND.

CHAPTER FOUR

FEATHERBEDS

*T*he threat to the company's racing reputation was growing again, with AJS winning the first 500cc world championship and the Italian four-cylinder Gileras demonstrably fast. Joe Craig's undying faith in the single-cylinder engine meant building a machine that could outmaneuver its faster rivals, through better braking and cornering. The answer to his prayers came in the form of an all-welded chassis that gave rigidity and lightness, and was destined to pass into legend — the Rex McCandless-designed Featherbed.

▼ GEOFF DUKE'S FIRST TT AS AN OFFICIAL FACTORY RIDER WAS THE 1950 JUNIOR, WHEN HE WAS SECOND TO THE EXPERIENCED ULSTERMAN ARTIE BELL. LATER IN THE WEEK, HE WON THE SENIOR RACE AT RECORD SPEED AND BEAT HAROLD DANIELL'S LAP RECORD THAT HAD STOOD SINCE 1938.

THE FACTORY'S RACING men were licking their wounds after the 1949 season. They had been knocked off their perch as world leaders when it came down to the real business of contesting an official world championship; they needed to get back in front of arch rivals AJS and to keep ahead of the threatening Gilera four-cylinder models.

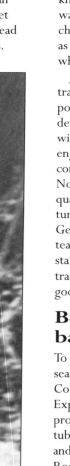

Ulsterman Rex McCandless, a friend of Artie Bell, offered a possible solution with his light, welded duplex frame. It was based on a design he had developed with a Triumph power unit, and Bell knew from personal experience how good that one was. Norton took on McCandless to produce the chassis that was to become known the world over as the "Featherbed" (Harold Daniell's description when comparing it with the 1949 frame).

Joe Craig had spent a lot of time getting the traditional single-cylinder motors to produce more power for 1950, part of his constant program of development. The brief cooperative association with ERA for the development of a four-cylinder engine had not progressed beyond the construction of a slave 125cc single-cylinder unit. Norton cautiously opted to stay with the known quantity of a single. But Joe Craig had a finely tuned eye for talent and agreed that the promising Geoff Duke could move up to a ride with the race team after he'd finished the winter trials. Duke started the year well with overall victory in the trade-supported Victory Trial. It seemed like a good omen.

Bob Collier joins the back-room boys

To get a fleet of the new models ready for the season, Craig recruited more help, and Bob Collier was taken on as a fabricator in the Experimental Shop. Collier's first job was producing gear and brake controls. After the light tubing was cut and bent, it was pinned to a board and taken to Arthur Westwood in nearby Asylum Road to be welded.

Collier recalled: "One day they were too busy to do Norton's bits quickly and Arthur said that Joe Craig would just have to wait. That caused a bit of a panic, so I said "I'll take them home and weld them if you like." They looked at me amazed and said "Have you got your own welding equipment?"

"Imagine it – this was the Norton factory and

◀ OFFICIAL PHOTOGRAPH TIME AT THE NORTON FACTORY WHEN THE NEW FEATHERBED WAS ANNOUNCED TO THE PRESS. THE PHOTOGRAPHER'S TRICK OF SHAKING A SHEET IN THE BACKGROUND MADE DETAIL CLEAR AND COVERED UP THE GRIMY OLD FACTORY BACKDROP.

they didn't have welding gear! The frames were all lugged and brazed then, so they didn't really need it. I brought my kit in and we used it for three months, but then I told Joe Craig that he'd have to get his own. He'd have let me go on forever if they didn't have to pay."

Early successes for the Featherbed

The first bikes were ready for their official debut at the military camp track at Blandford (Dorset) in April 1950. Geoff Duke, wearing a set of one-piece leathers that he had had tailormade to reduce wind resistance, won the race and broke the lap record. It was an historic occasion, the first win for a frame that is still made today and regarded as the very best of the classic era.

Artie Bell drove the point firmly home with a record breaking win in the Junior TT, and new team member Duke was second. Then it was Duke's turn, and he smashed all records in the Senior race, with a race average of 92.27mph and a best lap of 93.33mph. Harold Daniell's Senior TT record had at last been bettered – after 12 years!

▶ THE STYLISH GEOFF DUKE AGAIN, LEAPING AT BALLAUGH BRIDGE IN THE 1950 JUNIOR TT. DUKE'S SMOOTH AND SCIENTIFIC WAY OF RIDING KEPT THE TIME-WASTING JUMP TO A MINIMUM, AN ABILITY HE LEARNED AS A MEMBER OF THE ROYAL CORPS OF SIGNALS DISPLAY TEAM.

▲ TONY NORRIS, ON THE FAN NORTON HE BUILT HIMSELF WHEN REFUSED A FEATHERBED FOR THE TT, HEADS FOR 12TH PLACE IN THE 1953 SENIOR. FOLLOWING HIM OVER BALLAUGH BRIDGE ARE L. C. BUTLER (23) WHO FINISHED 11TH, AND CATCHING UP FAST IS FIFTH FINISHER BILL DORAN (AJS).

1952 500CC MANX RACER

SPECIFICATION

In 1951 the Featherbed frame was made available to racers for the 350 and 500cc Manxes, and in 1952 the engine was moved forward, with twin camshafts to set the style that would be developed until the model was withdrawn from the line in 1963. The Manx was the definitive 500cc racing motorcycle of the 1950s and 1960s, and its ability was so great that it remained competitive enough for Godfrey Nash to win the 1969

Yugoslav Grand Prix on a machine that many considered to be long out of date. The Manx remains the most collectable of all Nortons and is very competitive in the historic racing scene; the advantage of the high prices asked of collectors for good examples is that they make the manufacture of good-quality spares viable, so the bikes keep on racing. If ever a motorcycle was destined to be active forever, it is the Manx Norton.

ENGINE Air-cooled vertical single-cylinder, with two valves operated by twin shaft and bevel-driven overhead camshafts. 79.6mm x 100mm stroke = 498cc. Magneto ignition; Amal carburation. Compression ratio 8.67:1 (optional 13:1 alcohol piston available to special order). Dry-sump lubrication.

TRANSMISSION Primary and secondary drive by single-row chains, via exposed multi-plate dry clutch. Norton-built four-speed trnsmission with foot change; ratios 10.52, 6.0, 4.97, and 4.52 to 1.

FRAME AND SUSPENSION Reynolds 531 tubing duplex cradle with Roadholder front forks and swinging-arm rear.

WHEELS Spoked, with 19 x 3in (483 x 76mm) front and 19 x 3.5in (483 x 89mm) rear tires. Conical drum brakes, 8in (203mm) front, 7in (178mm) rear.

DIMENSIONS Wheelbase 56in (1422mm); seat height 30in (762mm). Fuel-tank capacity 6.3gal (24l); oil-tank capacity 1.2gal (4.6l).

WEIGHT 298lb (135kg).

POWER 37.5bhp at 6200rpm.

PRICE £429 6s. 8d.

Off to the continental Grands Prix went the team, ready to show the rest of the world the way at the Belgian meeting. The 500 race started disastrously for Norton, when Artie Bell tangled with Les Graham as they tried to avoid the erratic Carlos Bandirola and slid into a trackside commentary box; Bell never fully recovered from his injuries. Duke took the lead, sheer hard riding taking him ahead of the Gileras until the tread of his rear Dunlop stripped off the tire carcass and he limped into the pits and out of the race. At the Dutch it was the same story, but this time the lifting tire tread jammed under the rear mudguard and brought Duke off. Fortunately he was only bruised, but his championship chances seemed fatally damaged.

A change to Avon tires got Duke back to winning form for the Ulster GP, and he rounded off the season with a clear win from Umberto

Masetti's Gilera at his rival's home round at Monza. But the Italian had built up too many points with consistent finishes for Duke to catch him, and the crown of crowns went to Italy. However, Norton had a brilliant new star in their galaxy, and the Featherbed, powered by Craig's special engines, had a realistic chance of world success.

The Manx DOHC

The standard production double-camshaft Manx (the long-used informal title had been officially adopted after the war) was built with the Featherbed chassis in 1951, and every serious racer wanted one. Supplies were very limited, with the factory dependent on the Reynolds Tubing Company's welding output, and inevitably there were disappointed customers. And as it became apparent how good the bike was, the demand for it

grew ever more insistent. Most applicants, however, were disappointed. Tony Norris, a development engineer at the Rover car factory in Solihull, was told bluntly by Norton's Gilbert Smith that he was not fast enough to be one of the select few who could have a Featherbed for the TT. Norris was not easily put off, and arranged with a sympathetic boss to work nights at Rover and produce his own version of the new frame. With no frame jig available at the car plant, he bent the main tube members around the trunk of a tree in the factory grounds! In the 1953 Senior TT Norris on his FAN Norton was 12th. For 1954 he had a Featherbed.

Pip Harris was a fast-rising star in sidecar racing, one of the very few who could threaten Norton's official driver, multi-world champion Eric Oliver. Harris ordered one of the new Featherbeds for the 1952 season, only to be told that he could not take delivery until after the TT in June. As he had sold his old 596cc Norton, it left him without a bike for the opening of the season. He did a deal with the Vincent factory and appeared at the April Silverstone meeting with their "Gunga Din" 1000cc development bike hurriedly hitched to a Watsonian sidecar. During a mixed practice session, he passed Dave Bennett on a factory 350 down the straight, and in the handicap race he beat Eric Oliver. "Next week, there was a letter from Norton's saying my Manx was ready," Harris remembers with a quiet smile.

The Golden Year

1951 was the best year of all for the factory team, with Duke winning 350 and 500 TTs and then both world championships – the first man to win two world titles in one season. The dynamic Eric Oliver did it again in the sidecar class, to take his third successive title on a Norton; the factory also won the manufacturer's title in all three classes. Duke was a national hero, awarded the RAC's Segrave Trophy for driving achievement and voted

"Sportsman of the Year." He was the first motorcycling star of the post-war era to be widely known to the general public, and photos of the handsome Lancashire lad in his Norton crash helmet were in demand.

Fate isn't kind forever, however, and 1952 wasn't such a good year for Duke, even though he retained the 350cc world championship and was awarded the OBE for his services to motorcycling. Halfway through the season he fell in a non-championship race at the narrow and slippery Schottenring circuit in Germany and spent

thirteen weeks with his leg in plaster; Masetti on a Gilera-4 became 500cc champion again. Norton had the consolation of another Senior TT win, but it was a very close thing. Reg Armstrong was crossing the finish line under the checkered flag when his primary chain snapped and snaked off into the road. Once more, Norton's single was looking old-fashioned and seriously stretched in its efforts to stay with the opposition. The only exception was in the sidecar class, where factory tester Cyril Smith took over as champion after Eric Oliver missed races through injury.

The flying Rhodesian

Duke and Armstrong joined Gilera for 1953; significantly, Norton had been bought out by Associated Motor Cycles. To lead the race team in 1953, they promoted another brave new talent in Rhodesian Ray Amm, a deeply religious man. "You never heard him say anything at a prize presentation before he thanked God for looking after him," remembers Stan Hackett, who worked in the drawing office on Joe Craig's projects.

There was a forward-thinking development that year with a solo with the rider in a kneeling position, but it was banned by unbending officialdom at the TT. Ray Amm changed back to conventional bikes to join the select few with wins in both Junior and Senior races in one week, the Senior after a scrap with Duke on the Gilera of such intensity that Geoff fell. Amm took a tumble

◄ CYRIL SMITH WON THE WORLD SIDECAR CHAMPIONSHIP IN 1952 AFTER ERIC OLIVER CRASHED IN A MINOR RACE AND MISSED THE GRAND PRIX. IN THE SIDECAR AT THE GERMAN GP IS LES NUTT.

▲ SHEER DETERMINATION AND GRIT GOT SMITH TO SECOND PLACE IN THE ITALIAN GRAND PRIX AT MONZA, TO BEAT CHAMPIONSHIP RIVAL ALBERTO MILANI'S FOUR-CYLINDER GILERA.

◀ Eric Oliver, with his 1954 outfit, set a trend that was to last for decades, where the driver knelt on pads instead of sitting on a seat. Les Nutt was in the sidecar when he drifted his way to victory in the TT that year.

as well on the final lap, but picked the bike up and carried on, minus one footrest, to secure that precious win for Norton.

At the Dutch TT there was a shock when the new 350 Moto Guzzis just rode away from Amm and Australian Ken Kavanagh on the Nortons. In the 500 race, Duke's skill and the Gilera's speed were just too much, and he won from team-mate Armstrong. Ray Amm ran out of fuel – a miscalculation not at all typical of Joe Craig's usual organization. At the Belgian, Amm was second in

the 500 race to Milani's Gilera, after Duke retired. Then Amm fell when leading the 350cc French Grand Prix, breaking a collarbone, and any dreams of a solo world title for Norton were broken at the same time. But the ever competitive Eric Oliver kept the flag flying in the sidecar class to bring back one crown to Bracebridge Street.

The kneeler proved its ability with a record-breaking spree at Montlhéry, south of Paris, at the end of the season. In 1953 Ray Amm and Eric Oliver broke a total of 61 world records in the

350 and 500cc classes; it was a proud achievement to boast of at the annual Earls Court Show. Oliver, an original thinker in his constant quest for race-winning speed, recognized the advantage of the kneeling position, and in the following season he raced a fully streamlined outfit that set the trend for years to come.

1954 was to be the final racing fling for the factory in the Grands Prix, while the catalog Manx was given the benefit of racing experience with shorter stroke engines for both 350 and 500cc

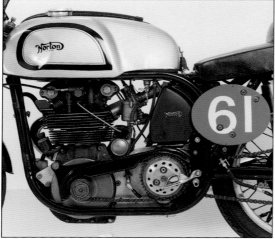

models. However, the International roadster, now using the Featherbed frame to compete with BSA's improving Gold Star, retained the traditional 79mm x 100mm measurements for the 500. The neglect of the Inter's development soon showed in the Clubman's TT races, which were dominated by the Gold Star from 1955.

Short-stroke racers

The 1954 works racers featured outside flywheels to accommodate very short strokes, the 500 now measuring 90mm bore x 78.4mm stroke. More obvious to the trackside fans was the distinctive streamlining, known as the "Proboscis" because of its long nose. It was designed in the Experimental Department, with a wire frame built around Ray Amm and covered with cardboard and paper stuck on with modeling clay, before airflow was tested with cigarette butts and an electric fan. Compared with Moto Guzzi's huge wind tunnel, it was all pretty crude, but the fairing worked.

Amm was well ahead in the 350cc TT until a

◀ PURE FUNCTION. THE TRANSMISSION IN THE 1954 OUTSIDE FLYWHEEL RACER WAS A FIVE-SPEED UNIT BY BURMAN, AND THE INCREASING SPEEDS WERE ADDRESSED WITH A FRONT BRAKE THAT USED AN EXHAUST FAN EFFECT TO DRAW COOLING AIR THROUGH THE HUB.

▲ THE 1954 DEVELOPMENT OF THE WORKS RACER WAS JOE CRAIG'S ULTIMATE ACHIEVEMENT. THE HARD WORKING EXHAUST VALVE WAS OIL-COOLED, THE FLYWHEEL WAS OUTSIDE THE CRANKCASES AND THE 350, MEASURING 78MM BORE X 73MM STROKE, GAVE 40BHP AT ITS BEST.

broken tappet stopped him. Then he took on Duke and the Gilera in the 500cc Senior, still the race that Norton rated above all others. Foul weather that had riders cornering with their feet down persuaded officials to stop the race after only four laps, when Amm was ahead of Duke. It was a controversial result, but Norton had another Senior TT win to their credit. Even better, the sidecar race had been revived, and Eric Oliver won it. His tally of four world titles made him the most successful Norton championship contender of all.

End of an era

Amm won the 350 and 500cc Ulster GPs and then the 350 German, but even his heroic riding could not keep the much faster Italian bikes at bay. Fergus Anderson on the Moto Guzzi won the 350 title, and Duke on the Gilera took the 500, but perhaps the most bitter and unexpected blow was Eric Oliver and Cyril Smith being beaten by Willi Noll's BMW twin for the sidecar crown.

Then came the shock announcement from Associated Motor Cycles, Norton's owner: there would be no more special factory racers in future; the company would concentrate on development

RAY AMM, ONE OF THE BRAVEST RIDERS WHO EVER SAT ON A MOTORCYCLE, WAS ALLOWED TO TRY THE EXPERIMENTAL 350CC KNEELER DURING 1953 TT PRACTICE. IT SHOWED PROMISE, BUT THE RULE BOOK WAS NOT VERY FLEXIBLE AND THE RACE AUTHORITIES EVEN LESS SO. THE BIKE DID NOT RACE.

IN THE 1954 SENIOR TT, AMM RODE THE DISTINCTIVE "PROBOSCIS" TO A CONTROVERSIAL VICTORY WHEN THE RACE WAS STOPPED AFTER FOUR LAPS, WITH GEOFF DUKE (GILERA) BEHIND HIM. BUT IN LATER ROUNDS OF THE WORLD CHAMPIONSHIP, SHEER SPEED TOOK THE OPPOSITION AHEAD.

of the catalog Manx models, and lessons learned by the works team would be applied to production models the following year. The factory racers were lined up in what the factory called the Bottom Experimental Department and left there.

Ray Amm quit to join the rising MV Agusta team in Italy — but was tragically killed in his first race for them. His wife Jill, a slim blonde with the ability to bump-start his bike, returned to Rhodesia and became the female motor-racing champion there; racing was clearly a family habit with them.

Norton recruited brilliant young talent in the form of the two Johns, Surtees and Hartle, to join with the experienced Jack Brett in carrying the Norton banner. They rode hard, but had no realistic chance of winning against the ever-stronger opposition. The best TT results were fourth places for Surtees in the Junior and for Brett in the Senior; their highest placings in the

JOE CRAIG (LEFT) AND TEAM MEMBER JACK BRETT CONFER AS THE TEAM PREPARES FOR THE 1953 TT. BRETT WAS SECOND BEHIND RAY AMM IN THE SENIOR RACE THAT YEAR.

DEREK MINTER, ONE OF THE FINEST MANX NORTON RIDERS, WAS THE FIRST MAN TO LAP THE TT COURSE AT 100MPH IN 1961. AT SHORT CIRCUIT MEETINGS, HE WAS ALMOST UNBEATABLE AND TEAMED WITH TUNER RAY PETTY TO KEEP THE MANX COMPETITIVE YEARS AFTER FACTORY PRODUCTION ENDED.

IN 1954 THE YOUTHFUL JOHN SURTEES JOINED THE TEAM AND GAVE JOE CRAIG A SATISFYING FAREWELL WHEN HE BEAT GEOFF DUKE AND THE GILERA-4 AT SILVERSTONE. A SCIENTIFIC RIDER IN THE DUKE MOLD, SURTEES WENT ON TO ACHIEVE THE UNIQUE WINNING OF WORLD TITLES ON TWO AND FOUR WHEELS.

Grand Prix were Hartle's pair of seconds in the Ulster, behind Bill Lomas on a fully streamlined Moto Guzzi single. Joe Craig had to look to Surtees' wins against Duke in two British races to get any real satisfaction. At the end of the year Craig retired, and Surtees left to join MV Agusta.

Joe Craig's departure signaled the end of a remarkable period. From his arrival as competition manager in 1929 to the day he was presented with the farewell gift of a mounted Manx conrod by the race department, Craig had worked himself and his staff hard in pursuit of success. He had built up a team of craftsmen around him, real characters. There was Ivor Smith, who looked after the test house and ran countless engines on the dynamometer. "He was addicted to Castrol R oil," remembers Stan Hackett. "Used to have a little in a pan on the stove giving off the fumes." And there was Charlie Edwards, who worked with the greatest of Norton's riders as a mechanic and

speaks of them with deep respect: "Great men, and I was proud to work with them," he recalls.

The late Freddie Frith knew Harry Salter, a top machinist in the 1930s, and remembered him as a man who "just wanted someone to say 'Thank you' for a job well done." Stan Hackett knew him as the piston maker in the 1940s and 1950s: "You could give him a block of alloy and he'd turn it into something like a work of art," he says. "And he wasn't doing just one – he had to make about thirty, remember."

Leon Kuzmicki was Polish and came to Britain during World War Two. He was employed as a humble cleaner until his engineering talent was discovered and Craig put him on engine development. When the racing department closed, Kuzmicki moved on to Coventry Climax, to work on racing-car engine development. Bill Clark was the cylinder-head specialist. And then there was engine builder Frank Sharratt – what a contribution to Norton's name he made over long years of service.

Craig was renowned as a hard taskmaster, but he had to be to achieve so much. "At times, I am sure I may have seemed a bit demanding and hard to please," he wrote to Stan Hackett early in 1956. "But it was all due to a burning desire to try and achieve the best result possible in the circumstances."

The Manx soldiers on

The Manx model remained in limited production as 350 or 500 cc racers for the private owner, but there was competition from AJS's lighter 7R 350 and its derivative, the Matchless G50. The Manx was generally outpaced in the grands prix, but Jack Brett was a surprise winner of the 1957 500 Belgian GP after Gilera rider Liberati was disqualified. In 1958 Geoff Duke had factory support for the Swedish GP and won both 350 and 500cc classes – but MV Agusta had chosen to miss that event.

▼ THE GREAT MIKE
HAILWOOD GAVE THE MANX
NORTON ITS LAST TT WIN IN
1961, AFTER PUSHING DUNCAN
HOCKING'S FOUR-CYLINDER
MV AGUSTA SO HARD THAT IT
STOPPED.

▷ THE BEST OF RACERS ON
MANX NORTONS MEANT CLOSE
RACING. DEREK MINTER (11)
AND MIKE HAILWOOD SHOW
HOW TO KEEP IT CLOSE AND
FAST AS THEY BATTLE FOR
HONORS AROUND THE LEAFY
CURVES OF OULTON PARK.

It would be three years before Phil Read and the great Mike Hailwood showed there was life in the old bike by winning the 1961 350 and 500cc TTs on Manxes prepared by Bill Lacey. Hailwood's pursuit of Gary Hocking on the MV Agusta was a TT classic, the four-cylinder Italian bike fading and then retiring as the very special Norton gave no quarter and kept up the pace; Hailwood averaged 100.6mph, the first "ton" TT average for a Norton, winning his third race that week.

It was a magnificent achievement by Mike "The Bike." But the performance of the Norton needs to be placed in context. At the same meeting, Honda's little four-cylinder 250cc lightweight lapped the Mountain Circuit at a staggering 99.58mph – only 3mph slower than Hailwood's fastest lap!

The production Manx was carefully improved, with Doug Hele working on a modest budget to get better reliability and more speed, but when Associated Motor Cycles announced the closure of Bracebridge Street in 1962 and the move of

1962 500CC MANX MODEL 30
(ALSO AVAILABLE AS 350CC MODEL 40)

The Manx Norton's production life ended in 1962, with the closure of Norton's famous works at Bracebridge Street, Birmingham. It was still the mainstay of 500cc racing, but the troubled parent, Associated Motor Cycles, was cutting out what they saw as uneconomical models, even though Mike Hailwood had won the Senior TT the year before. It still used the excellent Featherbed chassis, but was handicapped by its standard four-speed transmission; ambitious riders fitted the Austrian Schafleitner six-speed cluster to make life a lot easier in the heat of battle. But Norton could claim that the Manx was "the most successful standard-production racing machine in the world" because the model's history could be traced back to the Arthur Carroll design of 1930. At the end, its performance owed more to Doug Hele's careful development than to Carroll's design.

SPECIFICATION

ENGINE Air-cooled vertical single-cylinder with two valves, operated by twin shaft and bevel-driven camshafts. Cylinder barrel and head of light alloy, crankcases of elektron. Lucas racing magneto; Amal GP carburetor; dry-sump lubrication. 86mm bore x 85.6mm stroke = 499cc (76mm x 76.7mm = 348cc). Compression ratio 11:1.

TRANSMISSION Primary and secondary drive by single-row chain via exposed three-plate clutch and close-ratio four-speed transmission. Ratios 7.52, 5.63, 4.65, and 4.53 to 1 (350cc: 9.11, 6.81, 5.64, and 5.12 to 1).

FRAME AND SUSPENSION Featherbed duplex cradle built by Reynolds in Reynolds 531 moly-chrome tubing. Norton Roadholder telescopic front forks; swinging-arm rear suspension controlled by Girling units.

WHEELS Spoked, with light-alloy rims on elektron hubs. Tires 19 x 3in (483 x 76mm) front and 19 x 3.5in (483 x 89mm) rear (both models). Front brake twin 7in (178mm) drums with single leading-shoe operation; rear single leading-shoe in 7in (178mm) drum.

PERFORMANCE Maximum speed (500cc): c 130mph (209km/h); (350cc) 120mph (193km/h).

DIMENSIONS Wheelbase 56in (1422mm). Fuel tank 6gal (22.75l); oil tank 1.1gal (4.25l). Weight (500cc) 313lb (142kg); (350cc) 307lb (138kg).

POWER (500cc) 47bhp at 6500rpm; (350cc) 35bhp at 7200rpm.

▼ By 1966 the Manx was out of production, but racers like Ray Pickrell (7) knew they were still the best for a private entrant in 500cc racing. To prove his point, Pickrell overtakes Griff Jenkins' Dunstall Dominator twin.

Norton production to the Plumstead factory in southeast London, it seemed to be the end of the line. The 1963 batch of racers was the last to be built, and in 1966 the racing department's stock of both Nortons and AJS and Matchless machines was sold off to Colin Seeley. He in turn sold the Norton stock and manufacturing rights on to John Tickle, an ex-sidecar racer who built his own frame and offered 350, 500, and even 650cc

engines. But demand was not high, and the Tickle Manx faded from the scene, leaving independent engineers such as Ray Petty to carry on preparing race machines and commission essential spares.

▼ Ellis Boyce on Francis Beart's immaculate Manx. His best result was second in the 1962 Senior TT.

The Norton spares business

Petty's vision paid off. At his instruction, in 1987, his parts business was sold to the Summerfield Brothers of Somercotes in Derbyshire, who had made parts for him. Today Summerfield Engineering produces a full range of engine and transmission parts; a number of specialist suppliers build Featherbed frames, and others devote their time and skill to producing the remaining parts necessary to build a complete Manx Norton. Jerry and Roger Summerfield actively race a selection of four bikes, some of them original Bracebridge Street models, with their own production providing necessary replacements. Jerry was named British Classic Racer of the Year in 1991 and regards the Manx as a tough, reliable bike that lasts well and can win: "One of our chassis is a 1954 outside-flywheel one with one of our engines fitted," he recalls. "I hit a dog at about 85mph at Darley Moor and the bike went end over end and bent the frame (it didn't do the dog much good, either). But Ken Sprayson pulled it straight again, he didn't even have to put new tubes in, and we're still racing it."

Factory production of the Manx may have ended in 1963, but the legend was too strong to die; it is still very much alive.

CHAPTER FIVE

TWIN CYLINDERS: THE DOMINATORS

*T*he parallel twin cylinder engine was not loved by engineers, who found its vibration unacceptable. But the public were lining up to buy them when World War Two ended, and even conservative Norton could not ignore the demand. Their offering was the handsome Model 7, using well-proven cycle parts and offering the same power as the highly regarded 500 International single. The advantage was a more flexible engine and enclosed valve gear that meant cleaner clothes at the end of a journey.

A TREND STARTED in 1937 that was to dominate the design thinking of the British motorcycle industry for many years. Edward Turner's parallel twin was launched by Triumph as the "Speed Twin" and was an instant sales success, its neat styling combining with good performance. Norton, like other makers, was left behind: with only 350 and 500cc single-cylinder models to offer, the catalog was painfully restricted. The 1938 public announcement said it was cutting back on racing to concentrate on machinery development production for the military; but team member Freddie Frith, himself a successful dealer after retiring from competition, saw it differently. "They were in trouble," he insisted. "They couldn't sell their old side-valves to the public. People were buying the Triumph twin."

The needs of the military kept Norton busy through the 1939–45 war, and with the coming of peace there was a demand for every available motorcycle. So sales were buoyant, but the success of the twin was not forgotten, and Norton's designer Edgar Franks drew one for presentation to his directors. Franks' idea was an in-line engine,

in the style of the Sunbeam that the BSA Group was actively developing. The board wouldn't accept anything quite so revolutionary.

Launch of Model 7

Franks' colleague Jack Moore submitted his own idea, a conventional parallel twin with twin camshafts and with the cylinder-head retaining bolts passing through the barrels and down into the crankcases. What happened to Moore's design remains a mystery.

Some stories claim a prototype was built; others insist that it was never started. It certainly did not go into production. We do know that Bert Hopwood was appointed Chief Designer in 1947 and that his first brief was to draw up a twin. The result was the 500cc Model 7 "Dominator," launched at the 1948 Earls Court (London) Show shortly after Hopwood left to join BSA. The Model 7 design was distinctive with its widespread exhaust ports, allowing air to circulate around them, and with its single camshaft located across the front of the engine. Camshaft drive was by chain outboard of the half-time pinion gear, to reduce mechanical noise. Cylinder bore was

▲ EARLY DOMINATOR TWINS STILL LEAD AN ACTIVE LIFE IN HISTORIC RACING, LIKE THIS MODIFIED 750CC MODEL 7.

◄ THE DOMINATOR THAT NEVER WAS. JACKIE MOORE'S DESIGN FOR NORTON'S FIRST PARALLEL TWIN, BUT IT WAS DROPPED IN FAVOR OF THE MODEL 7.

▶ THE MODEL 7 DOMINATOR WAS PRESENTED AS A SPORTS TOURER, BUT IN TIME THE MOTOR WAS DEVELOPED TO SURPASS THE INTERNATIONAL.

MODEL 7 DOMINATOR

The Bert Hopwood-designed Model 7 Dominator was the first Norton twin for some 40 years, and the first of a line that has lasted through to the present day. It was Norton's contribution to the twin-cylinder fashion that spread in the 1940s, after Triumph's "Speed Twin" had shown the way in the late 1930s. But while Triumph developed its twin as a sporting machine, Norton's racing and trials reputation had been built around the single-cylinder style, so it presented the Dominator as a high-performance touring model.

It was a sweet motorcycle to ride, with little engine vibration – as with most 500cc parallel twins before the demands of the size-conscious American market demanded that the motor be stretched ever larger to satisfy performance demands.

SPECIFICATION

ENGINE Air-cooled parallel-twin with vertical cylinders; barrels and head in cast iron. Two valves per cylinder actuated by rockers and pushrods from a single camshaft transverse in front of the crankshaft line. Single Amal carburetor; ignition by Lucas magneto. Compression ratio 6.7:1.

TRANSMISSION Primary and final drive by single-row chain via multi-plate dry clutch in oil-bath primary chaincase. Four-speed Norton transmission with foot operation; ratios 5.0, 6.05, 8.85 and 14.88 to 1.

FRAME AND SUSPENSION Norton-built frame of lugged and brazed construction, full cradle with single top tube. Roadholder telescopic front forks; plunger rear suspension, changed to swinging arm for 1954.

WHEELS Spoked, 20 x 3in (508 x 26mm) at front and 19 x 3.5in (483 x 89mm) at rear. Single leading-shoe drum brakes to both wheels.

EQUIPMENT Lycett cushion seat with optional pillion seat and footrests. Lighting by Lucas; speedometer by Smith's.

PERFORMANCE *c.* 90mph (145km/h) top speed.

DIMENSIONS Wheelbase 54.5in (1384mm); ground clearance 6.5in (165mm), saddle height 30in (762mm); weight 440lb (200kg); fuel-tank capacity 5.4gal (20.5l).

POWER 29bhp at 7000rpm.

PRICE (1951) £220 19s. 11d.

66mm and stroke 77.2mm, making 497cc.

The engine was mounted in an ES2-type cradle frame, with Roadholder telescopic forks and plunger rear springing. Finished in the established Norton silver and black livery with black and red pinstriping to the shapely tank, it was a handsome machine in the Norton way – not slim and delicate in appearance like the Triumph, but characteristically muscular in the Norton style. Claimed power output was 29bhp at 6000rpm, a worthwhile improvement on the 500cc single-cylinder roadster's 21 at 5500.

Early production was reserved for export sales, and British customers had to wait until late in 1949 to take delivery of the first production Norton twin in nearly 40 years. It performed as well as the 500 International, with less oil spray to contend with, and was much quieter mechanically. It was the way ahead, whatever the hardened traditionalists among Norton's customers might say.

▲ THE BRAVE STYLE OF DAVE DOWNER ON PAUL DUNSTALL'S 650 DOMINATOR WON RACES AT BRANDS HATCH AND BROUGHT A LOT OF PUBLICITY TO DUNSTALL'S CUSTOMIZING SHOP IN SOUTH LONDON. BUT IN A FURIOUS BATTLE WITH DEREK MINTER, DOWNER FELL AND WAS TRAGICALLY KILLED.

◀ THE 1951 PROTOTYPE OF THE FEATHERBED DOMINATOR, THE MODEL 88. THE REAR SUBFRAME WAS BOLTED UP AT THIS EARLY STAGE, IN THE SAME FASHION AS THE FACTORY RACING MANXES.

▼ BY 1955 THE REAR SUBFRAME OF THE FEATHERBED WAS WELDED UP. THE BIKE CAME WITH A DISTINCTIVE METALLIC GRAY FINISH TO CYCLE PARTS, INCLUDING THE DEEPLY VALANCED MUDGUARDS.

Model 88

Inevitably the sporting prestige of the Featherbed frame was combined with the new twin-cylinder engine to add a luxury sports tourer to the range. Triumph and BSA had both added 650cc twins to their lines, so Norton needed to add a little spice to their own menu. A prototype was seen at the Dutch TT in 1951, and in November that year the company announced the "Dominator de Luxe," later to be known as the Model 88. The frame was a copy of the racing Featherbed, using mild-steel tubing instead of the chrome-moly Reynolds 531 of the real racers; the rear sub-frame was bolted on.

The prototype had included extensive enclosure of the rear wheel and a nacelle enclosing the headlight in a style that shouted "Triumph copy," but the final production version was more conventional, with bare frame and a headlight mounted in the traditional way. The arc-welded frame, produced at Reynolds Tubing, contributed to a claimed weight of 380 pounds against the established Model 7's 413 pounds. There was clearly a mysterious slimming campaign being conducted at Norton, because the claimed weight

of the Model 7 had come down by 27 pounds in the space of one year without major changes to the specification. But it was still the only 500cc British twin to weigh over 400 pounds.

Demand outstrips supply

The Model 88 brought a new standard of handling to the roadster and was in great demand. This proved to be a major problem for the company, with the world clamoring for the new Featherbed and the output limited. Sales manager Leslie

▼ THE DOMINATOR WAS ONE
OF THE MOST HANDSOME ROAD
MACHINES OF THE 1950S. ONLY
TRIUMPH'S SLIM AND GRACEFUL
TIGER 100 COULD MATCH IT
FOR LOOKS, BUT NEVER FOR
ROADHOLDING.

1953 MODEL 88 FEATHERBED DOMINATOR

SPECIFICATION

The Featherbed frame was first available on a road machine in 1952, when the Dominator 88 went on sale. It used the same frame as the world-beating racing machines, but for road use it was made from mild-steel tubing instead of the Reynolds 531 used on the racers. It furthered Norton's racing legend, with advertisements for the new model featuring one of the TT-winning racers in the background to convince the buyer that he could ride bikes similar to those used by heroes like Geoff Duke and Ray Amm. There was a premium to be paid for the top model of Norton's 1953 touring line – it was some £27 more than the old-fashioned Model 7 with the traditional chassis.

ENGINE Air-cooled vertical parallel-twin, with two valves per cylinder operated by pushrods. 66mm bore x 72.6mm stroke = 497cc. Compression ratio 6.8:1. Lucas magneto ignition; Amal carburettor.

TRANSMISSION Primary and final drives by single-row chain via multi-plate dry clutch in oil-bath primary chaincase. Norton four-speed gearbox with foot change; standard ratios 14.88, 8.85, 6.05, and 5.0 to 1.

FRAME AND SUSPENSION Reynolds-built welded mild-steel duplex cradle, with Roadholder front forks and swinging-arm rear.

EQUIPMENT Dual seat standard; lighting by Lucas dynamo; Smith's speedometer.

PERFORMANCE Maximum speed *c.* 90mph (145km/h).

DIMENSIONS Wheelbase 55in (1397mm); ground clearance 5.5in (140mm); seat height 31in (787mm); weight 393lb (178kg).

POWER 29bhp at 7000rpm.

PRICE £265 15s. 6d.

▲ THE DOMINATOR WAS SUCH
A FLEXIBLE ENGINE, THE WHOLE
BIKE SO EASY TO RIDE AND
MANUEVER AROUND TOWN,
THAT THE FACTORY ISSUED
PUBLICITY PICTURES
SUGGESTING THAT RIDING WAS
SO SIMPLE THAT EVEN A WOMAN
COULD DO IT. A FAR CRY FROM
THE ATTITUDE OF THE 1990s.

▶ PROFESSIONAL TESTERS MAKE
VERY BAD PILLION PASSENGERS,
BECAUSE THEY ARE SO USED TO
HAVING THEIR PERSONAL
DESTINY FIRMLY IN THEIR OWN
HANDS. VIC WILLOUGHBY,
ROAD TEST EDITOR OF THE
MOTOR CYCLE DISPLAYS THESE
SYMPTOMS ON THE BACK OF A
MODEL 7.

at work. Norton's sales people obviously wanted the company to get wholeheartedly behind the bought-in frame, at the expense of Norton's own, outdated frame-making facility. On the other hand, Hepburn was probably under instructions from his board to move more of the traditional models simply to keep all parts of the factory at least working, if not busy.

One aspect of the early Dominator 88 design did not impress the men in the Experimental Shop. For work on the power unit, they had to take the engine and transmission out as one piece – but the bike's center stand was bolted to the engine plates and so had to be removed before the engine and transmission could be lifted. The time-wasting problem was solved by welding two "ears" onto the bottom frame rails and mounting the center stand on them.

The traditional Frame Shop, where craftsmen built chassis in the traditional pinned and brazed-lug style, could not be adapted to the new technology that Reynolds Tubing had long mastered. The solution would be a swinging-arm frame, but there was an urgent need to get it ready and into the line – and the Norton drawing office was not accustomed to thinking in terms of short

Hepburn warned Bob Collier that Reynolds Tubing could produce only 70 Featherbed frames a week at its Tyseley factory, whereas Norton needed to sell 110 machines every week just to break even; the old-fashioned plunger-sprung models and the specially made rigid-framed versions weren't selling in large enough numbers to make that crucial difference.

Norton, in short, were in trouble as a direct result of their new model's success. Ken Sprayson of Reynolds has since confirmed that their factory had the capacity to produce more frames, having switched from wartime aircraft production through office furniture to motorcycle chassis. There may have been a touch of company politics

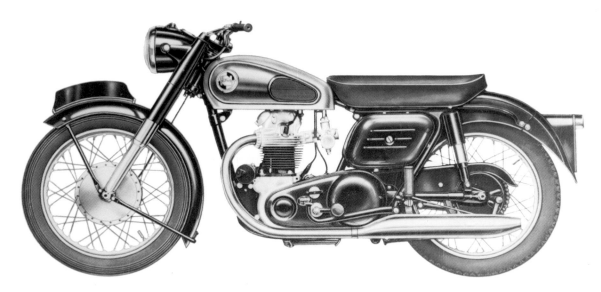

THE MODEL 77 WAS INTENDED AS A SIDECAR MACHINE. ITS LUGGED AND BRAZED FRAME CAME WITH SIDECAR ATTACHMENT LUGS, AND THE 600CC ENGINE FROM THE DOMINATOR 99 GAVE ENOUGH POWER FOR A GOOD PERFORMANCE. BUT AS SMALL CARS WERE BEING MADE, FEWER MODEL 77S WERE PRODUCED.

deadlines. Bob Collier, a stalwart of the Experimental Department and well used to the pressures that racing's needs imposed, volunteered to produce the necessary frame over a weekend. He was locked in on a Friday night with welding kit and a stripped machine, and by Monday morning had a swinging-arm ES2 on the bench for chief executive Gilbert Smith to examine. Smith looked it over and turned to designer Edgar Franks with the words: "Jolly good show, Edgar. It's a pity you didn't do it six months ago." Collier, who alone had done the work, just stood there amazed.

The AMC takeover

In the 1953 line, the Model 7 and the overhead-valve single-cylinder models were offered with a swinging-arm frame – but the company was weakened by the lost sales, and a takeover by the acquisitive Associated Motor Cycles was announced in February 1953. Norton became a

stablemate of AJS and Matchless of Plumstead, Francis-Barnett of Coventry, and James of Greet, nearby in Birmingham. Gilbert Smith of Norton and Donald Heather of AMC, a man with big ambitions for his group of companies and not given to listening to others, were never happy partners.

In 1956 the Model 99 de Luxe was announced, its 68mm bore x 82mm stroke giving it a capacity of 597cc; at the same time the old-fashioned Model 7 was dropped from the line. That meant sidecar enthusiasts could not for the moment have a new Norton twin hitched to their favorite Watsonian or Canterbury, as the factory actively discouraged fitting sidecars to the Featherbed. The solution to the problem came in 1957, when the Model 77 was launched with a frame from the factory's own shop that included sidecar-mounting lugs and the Model 99 engine to power it.

▲ THE 1957 DOMINATOR 99 OFFERED THE FEATHERBED FRAME FOR BEST HANDLING, A TRANSMISSION THAT WAS THE RESULT OF AMC-NORTON COOPERATION AND ONE OF THE BEST, AND A SET OF BRAKES THAT SET STANDARDS FOR OTHERS TO ASPIRE TO. A FINE ROAD BURNER.

◀ TRY THIS SORT OF MANHANDLING WITH A 1990S HEAVYWEIGHT MACHINE AND YOU COULD HAVE A BIG BILL FOR A BROKEN STAND, AT BEST, OR SCRATCHED BODYWORK IF YOU ARE UNLUCKY. MAYBE THE MAN IS TRYING TO SHOW HOW LIGHT THE DOMINATOR 99 IS?

SPECIFICATION

1956 600CC MODEL 99 DOMINATOR

In 1956 the Dominator line was extended with the introduction of the 600cc Model 99, with both bore and stroke increased from the long-established 500cc twin's dimensions. The extra capacity gave a modest power boost of just 1.5bhp, but the mid-range torque was much improved, and because of it the 99 was an easier machine to ride fast. Sidecar drivers quickly realized how flexible the new motor was and began to bolt sidecars to the Featherbed chassis; a Dominator 99 with the sleek German Steib single-seat sidecar became the ultimate sports sidecar outfit.

ENGINE Air-cooled vertical parallel-twin, with two valves per cylinder operated by pushrods. 68mm bore x 82mm stroke = 596cc. Ignition by Lucas magneto (after 1958, coil ignition on standard models); carburation by Amal. Dry-sump lubrication.

TRANSMISSION Primary and secondary drive by single-row chain, via multi-plate dry clutch running in primary-drive oil-bath. Norton transmission with foot change; ratios 12.2, 8.02, 6.04, and 4.53 to 1.

FRAME AND SUSPENSION Duplex cradle frame in mild steel, built by Reynolds. Norton Roadholder telescopic front forks; swinging-arm rear suspension.

WHEELS Spoked, steel WM2 rims. Tires 19 x 3in (483 x 76mm) front, 19 x 3.5in (484 x 89mm) rear. 8in (203mm) diameter single leading-shoe front brake, 7in (178mm) rear; both in full-width alloy hubs.

EQUIPMENT Lucas lights, powered by dynamo until 1958, then by Lucas crankshaft-mounted alternator. Ignition by Lucas magneto until 1958, then by coil on standard models. Instruments by Smith's.

PERFORMANCE Maximum speed c. 105mph (169km/h).

DIMENSIONS Wheelbase 55.5in (1410mm); ground clearance 6.75in (172mm); fuel tank 4.2gal (16l); oil tank 0.6gal (2.6l); weight 395lb (179kg).

POWER 31bhp at 5750rpm.

PRICE (1957) £283.19s.

ISDT Dominators

Soon after the twin's 1948 introduction, experiments had begun on preparing it for trials work. Four Model 7s were adapted for the factory's entries in the 1950 International Six Days Trial, held in Wales in a very wet September. Rex Young finished the week without loss of marks and won the only Gold Medal for Norton. Dick Clayton rode as one of Britain's B team and was reported to have filled his Dominator's engine with water when he followed another rider through a water splash and was caught in his wave. Dominator engines, like all others, do not run well on water; Clayton retired.

For 1951 the ISDT was held in Italy and the team, led by Rex Young, had Featherbed twins sporting conical front hubs similar to those of the Manx racers. They clearly prospered in the warm weather, and all finished without losing a single point to win a Manufacturer's Team Prize. In 1952 the trial in Austria was really tough, and not one manufacturer won a team award; Norton had two Gold Medalists, with Jack Breffitt and Don Williams (replacing an injured Rex Young) managing to get through without loss.

Bob Collier had built a Dominator engine into a 500T trials chassis as a test bike for the 1950 ISDT team. The team had finished the 1949 event with their single-cylinder big-ends rattling, and the twin was considered a better bet for a long, hard slog. When Collier was told that the twin wouldn't fit into the 500T frame, it was like a red rag to a bull. He simply took his welding torch to the front down-tube and bent it enough to make room for the twin-cylinder engine to slot into place. After testing this piece of instant adaptation, the team chose the sprung-frame option, clearly the better choice for six days of cross-country riding against a tight time schedule.

The rigid-framed twin stood unused until Collier, himself a top-flight trials driver, mated it with a sidecar. He first rode it in the 1953 Clayton Trophy trial in Derbyshire with trade plates fitted, and when a picture appeared in the press of a mysterious Norton twin, Gilbert Smith was less than pleased to see the company's trade plate on it (the insurance didn't cover competitive events). Collier pointed out that he had finished second in his class and had brought Norton publicity, so the prototype was properly registered, and in 1953 Collier used it well enough to win his class in the Cotswold Cup in the Stroud Valley, Gloucestershire, and the Red Rose Trial, Lancashire. Accepted sidecar wisdom of the time insisted that a twin would not work well in trials, and that a big single was essential for real grip on muddy sections. Collier's answer was succinctly expressed as "Start three fields back and let it rip."

▼ FEATHERBED DOMINATORS WERE USED BY THE FACTORY TEAM IN THE 1951 INTERNATIONAL SIX DAYS TRIAL. REX YOUNG, DICK CLAYTON, AND JACK BREFFITT ALL FINISHED WITH NO TIME PENALTIES AND WON A MANUFACTURER'S TEAM PRIZE FOR NORTON.

Oliver returns

The Model 77 was dropped from the line in 1958; it was never a big seller, and the official view that the Featherbed should not be fitted with a sidecar had been swept aside when maestro Eric Oliver came out of retirement and entered a Model 88 with a touring Watsonian sidecar in the 1958 TT. It seemed an impossible task, matching a standard road outfit against the best in the world, including the all-conquering BMWs. Admittedly the Oliver Norton was not quite standard, being fitted with one of the special close-ratio gear clusters made for earlier Daytona races, when Manxes had to be fitted with a kick-start to comply with the regulations. That change gave Eric the higher-ratio first gear he needed, but the rest of the outfit was basically standard; he even had the inexperienced Mrs. Pat Wise sitting in the sidecar, and not some agile veteran of the grand-prix circuits, to move vital weight around and help balance.

Oliver proved his point. He couldn't match the really serious front runners, but he clearly wasn't an old has-been wishing in vain for a miracle. The Dominator 88 outfit finished tenth and delighted the crowds as Oliver lifted the sidecar wheel over the curbs on lefthanders. He proved that talent like his lasts forever; more significantly, he removed any doubts about the Featherbed working with a properly fitted sidecar.

Production racers

In 1958 the Nomad was announced, using the Model 77 chassis but with its 600cc engine running a hotter camshaft, two-into-one exhaust, twin carburetors, and a higher compression ratio; claimed power output was 36bhp, a great deal sharper than the 31 gentle horses in the 77. Upright handlebars, knobbly tires, alloy mudguards, and a slim competition tank confirmed that this was an export scrambler, aimed at the American market.

Norton was clearly beginning to look at the sporting potential of the Dominator, and in 1961 came the 88 and 99SS variations, with twin carbs and sporting camshafts. Production racing was enjoying a revival, and Norton was a company with a racing pedigree. It was quietly developing the twins, and in 1960 Dennis Greenfield and Fred Swift from the factory rode a Dominator 88 to win the 500cc class in the Thruxton 500-mile race for production models.

◀ THE FACTORY DOMIRACER IN 1962, WITH THE VERY SPECIAL DOMINATOR 88 DEVELOPMENT ENGINE MOUNTED IN A CONVENTIONAL FEATHERBED FRAME INSTEAD OF THE MUCH LOWER BUILT LOWBOY FRAME USED BY TOM PHILLIS IN 1961

▲ BOB COLLIER, NEVER A SLAVE TO CONVENTION, RODE IN TRIALS ON A NOMAD TWIN WITH HIS OWN DESIGN OF LEANING SIDECAR, CONTROLLED BY A STEERING WHEEL IN THE PASSENGER'S HANDS. HOW THE PASSENGER FOUND TIME TO USE IT ON TERRAIN LIKE THIS IS NOT CLEAR.

The potential of the twin was confirmed at the 1961 Isle of Man TT, where a very special 500 with lightweight frame was ridden by Australian Tom Phillis in the Senior TT. That was a glorious day for Norton, with Mike Hailwood winning and Bob McIntyre second on single-cylinder Manxes, and Phillis third on the experimental twin after a lap at over 100mph. Doug Hele describes that ride as his outstanding memory of a non-British rider in his racing days: "Consider that he did one lap of practice and then went out and stayed with the very best," he says. "When he slowed down, it was the bike's fault, not his."

The single-minded commitment of a top racer is illustrated by Hele's memory of Phillis's ride on the twin at the Ulster Grand Prix later that year. "Tom came round on the first lap with Mike Hailwood and the MV. Phillis had got it into his mind that he was going to stay with him – but then the rain came down, and on the first bend he crashed. He said it was handling really well, but in the wet you can't throw them about." The twin wasn't seen again as a factory entry.

Slimline Manxman

1960 was the year the Manxman was launched, a 650 with a stroke of 89mm abut the same 68mm bore as the well established 600. It was fitted with upright bars in the American style of the day, but had twin down-draft carburetors, 8.3 to 1 compression, and a rev-counter drive hinted that there was something very different to come. It was, indeed, a sports bike looking for the right clothes before it appeared in public. Early in the same year, the Featherbed was modified, its top rails waisting in to give the rider greater comfort. This was the Slimline, and from that time on the older version was known as the Wideline.

▲ THE NOMAD WAS AN EARLY EXAMPLE OF ASSOCIATED MOTOR CYCLES PRACTICING BADGE ENGINEERING, WITH NORTON 600CC POWER AND AJS/MATCHLESS INFLUENCE EVIDENT IN THE CYCLE PARTS. IT WAS BUILT FOR THE AMERICAN OFF-ROAD MARKET.

▶ THE MANXMAN OF 1961 USED THE TWIN-CARBURETOR 650CC ENGINE IN THE FEATHERBED FRAME, WITH HIGH, WIDE HANDLEBARS OF AMERICAN PERSUASION

▼ THE 650SS WAS THE DEFINITIVE SPORTING MOTORCYCLE OF THE EARLY 60S, COMBINING HIGH POWER OUTPUT WITH EXCELLENT HANDLING. OTHER MAKERS MIGHT CLAIM MORE POWER, BUT NONE COULD MATCH THE NORTON FOR ALL-ROUND CAPABILITY. A TRUE CLASSIC.

checking a standard machine over carefully, even though Lawton did not tune for extra power, preferring reliability in a long race. The Lawton riders had reported handling problems, strange though that may seem with the Featherbed chassis, and the team finally cured it by having the wheels rebuilt to align them with the center of the machine's lateral weight distribution.

The 650SS was the ultimate sporting Featherbed twin for the road, but a bike of even more significance in Norton's history was the 1962 Atlas, the next development of the faithful old Hopwood design. By increasing the cylinder bore from 68 to 73mm, the 650 became a 750, and with the compression lowered from 8.9 to 7.6 and with a single carburetor, the whole character of the engine was changed. The Atlas came with a huge spread of power, a top-gear-only capability for cross-country journeys, and a chassis that was

Dominator 650SS

In September 1961 the 650SS was announced, with a stronger bottom end, thanks to larger big-end journals and a wider flywheel. Ignition was by magneto, reflecting racing tradition. Power output was 49bhp at 6800rpm, and top speed was very close to 120mph.

Down in Hampshire Syd Lawton – briefly a Norton team member until a dreadful practice crash at the TT ended his racing career – looked at the new 650, talked to old friend Hele, and put down his order (no bikes were supplied even to leading dealers free of charge). Lawton recruited the very fast Phil Read and reliable Brian Setchell to his team and started a run of three overall wins in the Thruxton 500-mile production race, from 1962 to 1964. The bikes were then withdrawn from competition only because the regulations limited production racing to machines up to three years old. It had not been a simple matter of

▶ PHIL READ, WINNER OF THE 1961 JUNIOR TT ON A MANX NORTON, TEAMED WITH BRIAN SATCHELL TO RIDE SYD LAWTON'S 650SS IN LONG-DISTANCE PRODUCTION RACES. IT WAS A WINNING TEAM, WITH VICTORIES IN THE THRUXTON 500 MILE AND SILVERSTONE 1000 KILOMETER EVENTS.

the best available. Its big problem was vibration, and the top speed of 115mph became academic once the revs began to climb toward the 6800rpm at which 49bhp was claimed; in fact, at anything above 5000 revs, vibration affected rider comfort quite seriously. The model was taken up by Paul Dunstall, who had made his name with a succession of Norton twin victories in short-circuit races, and was so highly regarded that he was sold all the 500cc Domiracer stock when the project was quietly dropped in 1962. Paul entered two Nortons in the Manx 750cc Production TT in 1968, and Ray Pickrell won the race.

The move to Plumstead

In 1962, as we have seen, Associated Motor Cycles announced that Norton was to leave its traditional home in Bracebridge Street and move south to Plumstead (London), where a reduced line of models would be produced alongside AJS and Matchless. One of the last despatches from the old works was a batch of 650SS Models for the Queensland (Australia) Police. The cops down under must have handed out quite a few more speeding tickets that year.

The transfer of production from Norton's traditional Birmingham home was not a happy one. Bob Collier received an urgent telephone call at Bracebridge Street, asking him to trace the multihead drill operator whose old machine was ruining crankcases as newcomers to the model tried to produce Dominators in its new home. Collier knocked on the redundant technician's door and explained how the drill was damaging the crankcases.

The technician thought it over for a moment and then asked: "Didn't they take the plank?" It turned out that the drill was so old that a plank of wood had to be held against the center spindle to prevent "chattering" as it did its job of precision drilling.

Ken Sprayson had a few problems at Reynolds,

◀ THE COMPANY FOLLOWED THE FASHION OF THE 1960S AND FITTED BIG, CAST TANK BADGES THAT LOOKED INCONGRUOUS ON A SLIM AND FUNCTIONAL MOTORCYCLE.

▼ WHAT BETTER REGISTRATION COULD YOU HAVE FOR A 1962 650SS? THIS APPROPRIATE NUMBER WAS NEGOTIATED BY THE SECRETARY OF THE BRITISH MOTOR CYCLE RACING CLUB, WHO USED HIS NORTON TO TRAVEL ALL OVER THE COUNTRY ON RACING BUSINESS.

▼ RAY PICKRELL RODE PAUL DUNSTALL'S 750CC ATLAS IN PRODUCTION RACES, AND HIS COLLECTION OF WINS INCLUDED THE 750CC

PRODUCTION TT. DUNSTALL FITTED HIS MODELS WITH NEAT TWIN DISKS, PREDATING THE FACTORY BY SOME YEARS.

1962 750CC ATLAS

The Norton Atlas was the starting point for the line of 750cc Norton twins that remained in production until 1975 and sold in many thousands all over the world. It became renowned for two things: its wide spread of power, and the vibration that accompanied enthusiastic use of its upper rev range. The boost in size came by simply increasing the bore of the 650cc engine from 68 to 73mm, with the stroke remaining at 89mm. The result was a bike with the ability to pull from 25 to 110mph in top gear. Add the roadholding of the Featherbed frame, and the Atlas became a machine for the experienced rider to cover ground quickly. The vibration at high engine speeds encouraged use of the motor's flexibility and helped fuel consumption. The early versions wore the traditional silver and black Norton livery, with chromed mudguards to set it off.

ENGINE Air-cooled vertical parallel-twin, with two pushrod-operated valves per cylinder. 73mm bore x 89mm stroke = 745cc. Compression ratio 7.6:1. Amal carburetor; ignition by Lucas magneto (capacitor system from 1967).

TRANSMISSION Primary and secondary drive by single-row chain, via dry multi-plate clutch in primary-chain oil-bath to four-speed Norton transmission. Right-foot change.

FRAME AND SUSPENSION Mild-steel duplex-cradle Featherbed frame, with Roadholder telescopic front forks and swinging-arm rear suspension.

WHEELS Spoked, with steel rims. Front tire 19 x 3.25in (483 x 83mm); from 1966 19 x 3in (483 x 76mm). Rear 18 x 4in (457 x 102mm).

EQUIPMENT Lucas lighting, powered by crankshaft-mounted alternator; Smith's instruments.

PERFORMANCE Maximum speed *c.* 110mph (177km/h).

DIMENSIONS Wheelbase 55.5in (1410mm); ground clearance 6.2in (157.5mm); seat height 31in (787mm). Fuel tank 3gal (11.4l), from 1964, 4.3gal (16.4l); oil tank 0.6gal (2.6l). Weight: 395lb (179kg).

POWER 49bhp at 6800rpm.

PRICE (1964) £359.

where the Featherbeds were still being made. "One of the Plumstead inspectors rejected a frame because it wasn't correct to the drawing," he recalls. "So the foreman made one that was – and the engine wouldn't fit in it!" It was a case of craftsmanship on the shop floor dealing with a problem, and the rule-of-thumb remedy never getting into the official records. Maybe the craftsman who kept the real specification in his head saw it as part of his job security.

AMC Folds

At Plumstead the 600 models were dropped and the 500 and 650 options were trimmed down, and within a year the first fruit of cross-breeding between brands emerged. It was a handsome combination of AJS/Matchless CSR frame with the 745cc Atlas engine, dressed up in street scrambler guise; the front forks and wheels were Norton

type. Clearly intended for the American market, it joined the Atlas Scrambler for the very strong and brave to ride in desert races and enduros. In a further badge-engineering exercise, AMC offered 745cc scramblers with AJS, Matchless, or Norton on the tank.

Times were getting harder for the group, however, and after a series of boardroom shuffles and disputes, the bank foreclosed in 1966 and a receiver was appointed. The US agents, Berliner Corporation, tried to negotiate a rescue package, but the group was sold to Manganese Bronze Holdings, London. The 500 was dropped from the line, and as a slow and painful recovery got under way, the only twins to survive were the 650SS, the Atlas, and its AMC cousins. There was a brief life from 1967 to 1968 for the P11, using the 750 motor with twin carburetors in the AMC scrambler-cycle parts. Another short-lived model

was the Mercury, a single-carburetor version of the 650SS; it was intended as a stopgap until a new model could be put into production, but in fact it was made from 1967 to 1970 as the new design was sorted out. 1970 was the final year of the Featherbed twins, ending a production span of 18 years that had added to the company's reputation with the sporting rider.

◀ THE ALTERNATIVE TO THE P11 WAS THE RANGER, A SIMILAR COMBINATION OF CYCLE PARTS WITH THE SAME POWER UNIT. IT WAS POPULAR ON AMERICAN DESERT AND FIRE-ROADS WITH THE MORE MUSCULAR RIDERS. ONE OF THESE IN FULL FLIGHT DOWN A FOREST ROAD NEEDED A BRAVE MAN IN CHARGE.

▲ THE NORTON P11 WAS BUILT AT AMERICAN IMPORTERS' REQUEST, COMBINING THE WELL PROVEN AJS/MATCHLESS CROSS-COUNTRY CYCLE PARTS WITH THE BIG TORQUE OF THE 750CC ATLAS MOTOR. IT COULD NOT OFFER THE PRECISE HANDLING OF THE FEATHERBED CHASSIS, BUT IT WAS GREAT FUN.

CHAPTER SIX

THE COMMANDO

*T*he Commando could only succeed. Its use of rubber bushes to isolate the rider from engine vibration won it a design award, and its smoothness and rideability won the hearts of the riding public in Britain, who voted it Motor Cycle News *Machine of the Year five years in a row. It sold well in the United States, where its unhurried way of moving fast and low-speed pulling power was appealing as an alternative to the high-revving Japanese engines.*

WHEN MANGANESE BRONZE Holdings acquired the failed Associated Motor Cycles Group in 1966, chairman Dennis Poore realized that the public needed to see a significant development if they were to believe there was any future for Norton and the other famous old names in the AMC fold. The group had already acquired Villiers Engineering of Wolverhampton, and the new company that emerged from this was called Norton-Villiers. The only brands to continue in production were AJS, with two-stroke moto-cross models, and Norton with its twins.

Poore recruited talent to address the matter of something new from Norton. Bernard Hooper, responsible for the successful Villiers 250

"Starmaker," came back from self-employment and teamed with his old workmate Bob Trigg; from Rolls Royce came Dr. Stefan Bauer to take overall control of development and design. The team briefly considered the 800cc overhead-camshaft P10 that had been built at Plumstead, but its complexity and modest power offered too great a challenge. Instead they looked at the 745cc Atlas motor, powerful but far too vibratory, and considered how to adapt this simple unit for use in a new motorcycle.

New engine mountings

Hooper came up with the solution in a design that was to earn him a £1000 Castrol award for its effectiveness. The engine, transmission, and swinging arm were all isolated from the main chassis by rubber-bushed mountings at the front of the crankcase, cylinder head, and transmission cradle. The good news was that they left the rider free from vibratory aggravation at normal engine speeds. The bad news was that the bushes had to be adjusted by shimming after 5000 miles, otherwise roadholding deteriorated rapidly. It was a solution that Castrol may have admired for its ingenuity, but it was one that private owners and mechanics never learned to love.

The upper frame member was a single 2.25-inch 16-gauge tube with a duplex cradle sweeping elegantly around to a triangulated rear section. Roadholder forks and the 8-inch drum brake from the faithful Atlas were known quantities, and a handsome alloy primary chaincase housed the triplex chain-drive to a diaphragm clutch especially developed by Laycock Engineering. The up-rated 745cc engine, breathing more efficiently through twin Amal Concentric carburetors, tilted forward in an aggressive angle that was echoed by the down tubes of the main-frame cradle and the rear-suspension units. An elegant 3.9-gallon tank was gripped by extensions of the dual-seat side panels in the manner of good old-fashioned knee grips, but the overall effect was right up to date. Shown at the 1967 Earls Court Show, it was finished all over in silver with the distinctive seat in orange. Named the Commando, it was the show stopper.

Commando in production

Production started in Plumstead in 1968, and immediately a problem with the frame emerged. Ken Sprayson of Reynolds Tubing, who made the chassis, remembers it well: "The early ones had a very stiff gusset at the steering head, and they broke there. The first 100 bikes went to America and they were in trouble with them." Sprayson was consulted and offered a modified gusset, but Stefan Bauer insisted that heavier-gauge tubing was the solution. In a side-by-side test over the pavé at

▶ THE MESSAGE THIS SULTRY PAIR WAS SUPPOSED TO RELAY WAS THAT IN THE 1970S A COMMANDO FASTBACK WAS QUITE ACCEPTABLE OUTSIDE SUCH AN IMPRESSIVE HOME.

750CC COMMANDO

The 1967 launch of the Commando was quite a sensation: it signaled the arrival of a big British twin that did not trouble its rider with uncomfortable vibration. Ingenious use of rubber mounting insulated the rider from the problem. The model was an immediate hit and was voted Machine of the Year five years in a row by *Motor Cycle News* readers, who clearly liked its slim good looks and smoothness. It did not have quite the precision of handling that the Featherbed offered, but it was certainly good through the corners if the owner kept the rubber Isolastic bushes properly adjusted. As an exercise in taking long-established components and dressing them up in a choice of new clothes, the Commando, from the early Fastback through to the sporting John Player Replica, showed how to do it well.

SPECIFICATION

ENGINE Air-cooled inclined parallel-twin, with two pushrod-operated valves per cylinder. 73mm bore x 89mm stroke = 745cc. Compression 8.9:1. Lucas capacitor ignition; twin Amal carburetors.

TRANSMISSION Primary by triplex roller chain; secondary by single-row chain via dry diaphragm clutch in cast-alloy primary chaincase and oil-bath. Ratios 11.2, 7.45, 5.3, and 4.38 to 1.

FRAME AND SUSPENSION Tubular-steel duplex cradle with single top tube; swinging-arm rear suspension; engine and transmission remotely mounted on Isolastic rubber bushes. Roadholder telescopic front forks.

WHEELS Spoked, steel rims. Front tire 19 x 3in (483 x 76mm), rear 19 x 3.5in (283 x 89mm). 8in (203mm) twin leading-shoe front brake (from 1972 10.7in [272mm] disk brake); 7in (178mm) single leading-shoe rear.

EQUIPMENT Dual seat as standard; Lucas alternator lighting system; Smith's instruments.

PERFORMANCE Maximum speed *c.* 115mph (185km/h). Standing start 440 yards (402m) *c.* 13.5 sec.

DIMENSIONS Wheelbase 56.8in (1443mm); ground clearance 6in (152mm); seat height 31in (787mm). Weight: 398lb (181kg).

POWER 56bhp at 6500rpm.

Chobham (Surrey) test circuit, the solution emerged: the original design lasted just 12 laps before it fractured; a heavier-gauge version did 120 laps and gave up, while Sprayson's gusseted version did 300 laps without any sign of a problem. The experienced motorcyclist's view prevailed, and there were no more problems on that score.

In 1968 production was rolling and public reception was good enough to vote the newcomer *Motor Cycle News* "Machine of the Year" for the first of five years in a row. Initial output was from the old Plumstead works, but continued for little more than a year before development plans persuaded the company to move assembly to a brand new factory at Andover (Hampshire). The

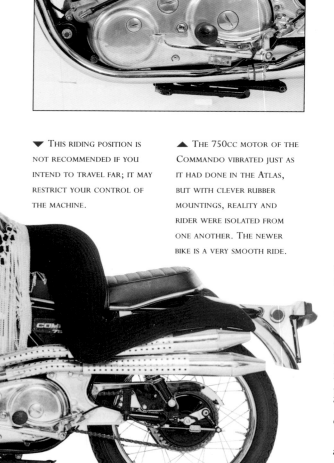

▼ THIS RIDING POSITION IS NOT RECOMMENDED IF YOU INTEND TO TRAVEL FAR; IT MAY RESTRICT YOUR CONTROL OF THE MACHINE.

▲ THE 750CC MOTOR OF THE COMMANDO VIBRATED JUST AS IT HAD DONE IN THE ATLAS, BUT WITH CLEVER RUBBER MOUNTINGS, REALITY AND RIDER WERE ISOLATED FROM ONE ANOTHER. THE NEWER BIKE IS A VERY SMOOTH RIDE.

engines and transmissions were to be built at the Villiers works in Marston Road, Wolverhampton, and trucked 120 miles south to the new factory. Bill Colquhoun had been in charge at Plumstead, and when manufacture ceased there, he was packed off to head the new Norton-Villiers Corporation in Long Beach, California, with $10,000 in the bank and clear instructions not to spend it unwisely. The American market was growing fast, and Dennis Poore wanted a foot in that vital area.

Peter Williams at Thruxton

The Commando engine produced 56bhp at 6500rpm, the bike was good for an honest 115mph, and its sporting appeal was obvious. A test department was established at Thruxton circuit, near the Andover factory, and among the staff was talented young Peter Williams, a brilliant development engineer and road racer. Williams' first job was preparing a Commando for the 1969 750 Production TT, but the ride was taken over by Paul Smart after Williams was injured in a racing crash. Smart finished second to Malcolm Uphill's record-breaking Triumph Bonneville at the Commando's first TT.

Williams rode the bike in the TT the following year, but again Uphill got to the flag first. His Triumph was slowing, and Williams passed him on the fast run down from Craeg-ny-Baa on the final lap, but the Commando hesitated with momentary fuel starvation and the determined Uphill was past. The Norton's victory in the 500-mile Thruxton production race must have seemed poor consolation.

In 1971 a Formula 750 racing Commando appeared, and Williams rode it to third place in the new class at the Isle of Man TT; he was leading the production 750 race until the ignition failed. But the team was doing well, they were attracting a lot of press interest and were a natural for John

seconds, 7.93, 7.93 again, and 7.95 to win the final. In 1976 he won again, with a time of 7.94.

Three stock-looking 750S models impressed on the West Coast road race scene, with George Kerker, Bill Manley, and Jack Simmons riding as "The Norton Gang" and consistently beating Japanese competition that could not live with the agile Nortons through the twisties. Norton were never a dominant force in terms of sales volume, and Mike Jackson estimates that they had a modest one percent of the market; but they certainly were good at making the headlines.

Player Cigarettes' sponsorship of their efforts in 1972, when world champion Phil Read joined Williams.

Transatlantic winners

Competition success was coming Norton's way in the United States, too, where Mike Jackson had taken over the West Coast office and made some useful contacts. "One day C. R. Axtell came to see us and said he'd like to get involved with Norton," he recalls. "We were such a small operation compared with BSA-Triumph and it was rather like Doug Hele going to Panther!" The cooperation was a fruitful one, and Jody Nicholas, Dave Aldana, and Alex Jorgensen on their Axtell-tuned

Ron Wood Nortons were almost unbeatable at the popular Ascot Park oval track in Gardena (Los Angeles). In August 1971 Nicholas won the Yamaha Gold Cup, which must have been a sweet victory.

The Norton name was gaining ground in the drag-racing scene, too, with Tom Christenson of Kenosha, Wisconsin, riding a double-engined 1620cc monster built by John Gregory. His bike used a unique two-speed transmission based on a Rambler overdrive unit and gave the *Hogslayer* an amazing lift in speed halfway down the track. The sheer consistency of Christenson's riding is best shown by his four quarter-mile runs to win the 1975 World Finals at Ontario, California: 7.99

▲ IN 1970 THE THRUXTON EXPERIMENTAL SHOP ADDED THE PRODUCTION RACER TO THE LINE, OFFERING AMBITIOUS RACERS THE CHANCE TO GET EVEN IN THE POWER RACE WITH THE RAPID THREE-CYLINDER TRIUMPH TRIDENTS.

▲ PETER WILLIAMS WAS AN INSPIRATIONAL TEAM LEADER, A VERY CAPABLE DESIGNER, AN ORIGINAL THINKER, AND AN INTERNATIONAL-CLASS RACER. HIS POLICY OF "ADD LIGHTNESS" AND BRILLIANT RIDING EXTENDED THE 750 NORTON'S RACING LIFE.

Police Nortons

Back in Britain, Neale Shilton had joined the team at Andover after resigning from the troubled BSA-Triumph group. Shilton was a one-man selling campaign, aimed at the police; he built up the first Interpol model despite a lack of cooperation from some of the production people, and set about riding it around Britain and booking business. At its peak, Norton's police business covered 48 authorities in Great Britain alone, and reached across to Greece, Jamaica, Kuwait, and Nigeria.

A man who lived with Norton's Interpol at the sharp end was Frank Parson, motorcycle technician at the Cheshire constabulary's Bromborough depot (south of Birkenhead), where he was responsible for a 15-bike mixture of Nortons and Triumphs. "Reliability was not wonderful," he remembers of the Interpols. "We had problems with head gaskets blowing, exhaust pipes snapping, the clutches would sometimes slip and drag, and we had troubles with the swinging-arm spindles wearing badly. We also had problems with the main bearings initially; they had a roller on the drive side and ball-type on the drive, and we were getting about six thousand miles life on average. I fitted two roller bearings, shimmed them accurately, and that was the end of the problem – they just went on and on."

▲ TOM CHRISTENSON, FROM KENOSHA, WISCONSIN, DOMINATED AMERICAN DRAG RACING IN THE 1970S WITH HIS "HOGSLAYER." TWO 810CC COMMANDO MOTORS DROVE THROUGH A MODIFIED CAR TRANSMISSION TO AN EIGHT-INCH WIDE REAR TIRE. 170MPH IN LESS THAN EIGHT SECONDS WAS THE RESULT.

▶ INTERPOLS BEING ASSEMBLED IN THE CROWDED WOLVERHAMPTON FACTORY, READY FOR POLICE PATROLS TO CHASE THEIR CIVILIAN COUSINS IF THEY GOT OUT OF LINE.

▼ THE 1976 MARK III
INTERPOL REFLECTED
DEVELOPMENT WORK WITH
MANY POLICE FORCES, BUT THE
INSPIRATION BEHIND THIS VITAL

WORK WAS NEALE SHILTON,
WHO HAD GONE TO DO THE
SAME JOB AT BMW. THE
TROUBLED NVT GROUP
STRUGGLED TO SUPPLY ITS
PATRIOTIC CUSTOMERS.

▼ THE INTERPOL WITH ITS
FLASHING BLUE LIGHTS
STRUCK TERROR INTO THE
HEART OF OFFENDING DRIVERS
WHEN THEY HEARD THE SIREN
AND REALIZED THAT THEY WERE
ABOUT TO BE CAUGHT.

Parson cured the head-gasket problem with some special solid copper ones made for him at the Cammell-Laird shipyard, but the later composite version from the factory proved to be even better. He also had a problem stemming from the police habit of regularly cleaning the bikes: "The engine mounting shims weren't lasting. The bobbies used a pressure hose, and when we took them apart there were no shims, just rusty dust!"

Quality control

The Commando had problems with quality when assembly at Andover used some inexperienced labor, but there was also commercial pressure at the Wolverhampton factory that resulted in corner-cutting simply to get units out and make the figures look good. Bob Rowley joined them as

a tester in 1972, when the highly tuned 65bhp Combat engine was coming into production, and had three crankshafts snap during his first week at work. "I went down the line and checked, turning the engines over, and you could hear the valves clicking as they hit the pistons. They were simply told to ease the tappets off! The company were on Export Credit Guarantee payments, so they were just exporting the problems." The Combat engine was an expensive mistake, and its fragility was finally cured with a little detuning and the fitting of Superblend main bearings that tolerated the whip in the hard-working crankshaft. 1972 was also the year the disk front brake was introduced an improvement on the 8-inch drum brake that soon became a commercial necessity.

The JPS Commandos

The sporting side got better in 1972. The John Player Nortons in distinctive blue and white went to Daytona, and Read came home fourth, after clocking 152.5mph on the banked section of the track. He then headed for Imola in Italy and gained another fourth place before the team packed the truck for the Isle of Man, where Peter Williams continued his second-place habit in the Production race. The big race for John Player was the F750, but there Williams, Read, and new team-man John Cooper all retired. At Thruxton, which was their home base and where defeat would have been very embarrassing, the team were first and second in the 500-mile race.

The engine's big spread of power also appealed to sidecar moto-cross enthusiasts, and it became the obvious successor to the 650 Triumph that had dominated in the 1960s. Robin Rhind-Tutt's Wasp

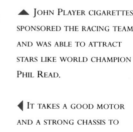

▲ JOHN PLAYER CIGARETTES SPONSORED THE RACING TEAM AND WAS ABLE TO ATTRACT STARS LIKE WORLD CHAMPION PHIL READ.

◀ IT TAKES A GOOD MOTOR AND A STRONG CHASSIS TO STAND THIS TREATMENT. EUROPEAN CHAMPIONS ROBERT GROGG AND ANDREAS GRABER IN FULL FLIGHT ON THE 750 NORTON-WASP.

chasssis with 750 Commando became standard competitive wear and won countless races. It was used by Swiss charger Robert Grogg to win five European championships, while in Britain Nick Thompson's domination of the domestic scene was finally ended by northerner Terry Good on a Yamaha. Good promptly switched to Norton power and carried on the Commando domination.

To prove how effective the Commando was as a private owner's racer, Richard Negus prepared his own machine and entered the two Peters, Davies and Lovell, in the 24-hour production race at Spa-Francorchamps (Belgium). "No one believed a Norton would last 24 hours," Lovell smiles at the memory. "The bike had finished second in a 600-kilometer (372-mile) race in Holland two weeks before, but we just changed the gearing and checked it over. We finished second, behind a works Honda, and averaged over 100mph. Richard Negus is one of the best blokes I've ever known for putting an engine together — it wasn't wild, but it was very, very reliable."

Events outside Norton that were destined to have dramatic effects were unfolding at this time, with the BSA-Triumph group in deep crisis and the Department of Trade and Industry making a rescue package conditional on a merger with Norton. Their destinies were joined, and together they would sink or swim. It was soon apparent that BSA-Triumph would not prove to be good swimmers, so the new Norton-Villiers-Triumph group was heading for big problems.

The 850 Commando

1973 was the year the 850 was launched. Actually 828cc, it used a 77mm bore instead of the 750's 73mm and came in a milder state of tune, with compression at 8.5 to 1. The factory addressed the problems — evident in the Combat's troubles — inherent in trying to stretch a 25-year-old design 500 to 750cc (and beyond) while trying to compete with more sophisticated Japanese four-

▼ THE MARK IIIA
COMMANDO REFLECTED SOME
SOUND DEVELOPMENT WORK,
AND QUALITY PROBLEMS WERE
BEGINNING TO RECEDE. FOR
MANY, THIS IS THE BEST OF THE
COMMANDOS AND STILL
PRACTICAL FOR THOSE WHO
PREFER THEIR MOTORCYCLES
NICELY MATURED.

1975 828CC MKIIIA COMMANDO

The Commando grew to 830cc in 1973, when the engine was up-rated with stronger crankcases and the bore increased to 77mm; the stroke remained the 89mm that dated back to the 650 model of 1960. It was a big motor to ask an electric starter to spin over, especially on a cold winter morning, and the novelty of press button starting proved to be a rare treat in reality. The bigger engine was fitted with a higher-ratio top gear in 1974 to make high-speed cruising even more relaxed; the disk front brake was as good as most available at the time, and the bigger Commando built up a loyal following.

ENGINE Air-cooled inclined parallel-twin with two pushrod-operated valves per cylinder. 77mm bore x 89mm stroke = 830cc. Compression ratio 8.5:1. Twin Amal carburetors; Lucas coil ignition.

TRANSMISSION Primary by triplex roller chain, secondary by single-row chain, via diaphragm dry clutch in cast-alloy oil-bath primary chaincase. Left-foot gearchange; ratios 11.20, 7.45, 5.3 and 4.38 (4.19 in 1974) to 1.

FRAME AND SUSPENSION Tubular-steel duplex cradle with single top tube. Swinging-arm rear suspension; engine and transmission remotely mounted on Isolastic rubber bushes. Roadholder front forks.

WHEELS Spoked, with steel rims. Tires 19 x 4.1in (283 x 104mm) front and rear. 10.7in (272mm) single disk front brake, 7in (178mm) rear drum until 1975, when 10.7in (272mm) disk used.

EQUIPMENT Dual seat; crankshaft-mounted Lucas generator; Lucas lighting.

PERFORMANCE Maximum speed c. 115mph (185km/h). Standing start 440 yards (402m) c. 14.2 sec.

DIMENSIONS Wheelbase 57in (1448mm); ground clearance 6in (152mm); seat height 32in (813mm). Fuel tank 3gal (11.4l) (Roadster); 6.3gal (23.9l) (Interstate). Oil tank 0.75gal (2.8l).

WEIGHT 415lb (188kg); 430lb (195kg) for Interstate.

POWER 60bhp at 6200rpm.

PRICE £1,161.00.

cylinder power, and the 850 came with the up-rated bottom-end and through bolts from cylinder head to crankcase. Claimed power was 60bhp at 6000rpm, and the big motor's easy manner of cruising won it many friends. If you wanted revs and reliability, you bought Japanese; if you wanted torque and unfussed cruising, you bought Norton.

The 850 could also be made to go fast. Factory tester Dave Rawlins built a reputation for being unbeatable in stock-class drag races in Britain on a bike prepared by John Baker. In one well-publicized demonstration, a stock 850 motor was run in, then tuned in the factory-approved way; with a big 24-tooth sprocket on the transmission and a small fairing to cheat the wind, it averaged 142.7mph over two runs through the quarter mile. It was then geared down with a 19-tooth sprocket, and on the sticky surface of Santa Pod dragstrip, it covered the standing start 440 yards in 12.00 seconds. Very impressive, but few believed that what they could buy in the showroom was anything like one of John Baker's special engines.

Return to the Midlands

The strange logistics of engines built in the Midlands and machines assembled in the South were overcome when all manufacturing was moved to the Wolverhampton site early in 1973. There was an improvement in machine quality with this easier control, and the Commando continued its process of steady improvement. The move to vernier adjustment of the Isolastic engine mountings made life a lot easier for both amateur and professional mechanics. But the cost of developing and tooling up for the 850 engine reflected adversely in the balance sheet that year.

This had little effect on the racing team, with John Player funds to help with the bills and a monocoque chassis from Peter Williams' drawing board. The machine overheated at Daytona, but in the Anglo-American Match Races, Williams won three of the six races to emerge as top scorer from the annual contest.

In the Isle of Man there was a bitter disappointment, however, when Williams retired while leading the 750 production race; but in the Formula 750 event, his deep knowledge of the circuit and the excellent handling of his own chassis gave him the TT win for which he had striven so long and so hard. It was no fluke either, it did not depend on rivals retiring, and it was crowned with a new record speed of 105.4mph. It was Peter Williams' finest hour.

Cosworth power

The team concentrated on Formula 750, their sponsor's priority, for 1974. But there was tension emerging, starting with the imposition of a tubular frame in place of Williams' preferred (and well-proven) monocoque. A short stroke engine, 77mm bore x 80.4 stroke, was ready for the TT, but Williams and new team-mate Dave Croxford were out within two laps. There was a new power unit

THE 828CC COMMANDO ENGINE IS THE BIG, UNHURRIED HEART OF THE MOTORCYCLE. IT STILL ENJOYS A FULL SPARE-PARTS BACK-UP, AND DEALERS LIKE FAIRSPARES OF STAFFORDSHIRE ARE CONTINUALLY WORKING TO IMPROVE IT FURTHER.

IN 1975 THE JPN COMMANDO HONORED THE TOBACCO COMPANY'S SUPPORT OF THE RACING TEAM IN ITS LIVERY AND

STYLE ON A STREET MACHINE. MANY REPLICAS HAVE BEEN BUILT, BUT ORIGINAL AND GENUINE JPNS ARE VERY RARE.

under development at Cosworth Engineering in Northampton, based on two cylinders of their long-lived, world-championship-winning 3-liter DFV V8 Formula 1 car engine. It was talked about in the town, and one rumor to emerge suggested that the team was struggling with the 360-degree crankshaft layout that Dennis Poore insisted upon instead of the 180-degree crank their experience suggested should be used. Poore had apparently told the Cosworth men that his motorcycle was not going to sound like a Honda and so a 360-degree crank it would have to be!

At the end of the season, Williams had a dreadful crash at Oulton Park (south-east of Liverpool). He clung to life for weeks before recovery began, but his racing career was over. John Player announced at the end of the season that its sponsorship would not be renewed, but the company bit the bullet and carried on with the new Cosworth "Challenger," despite the NVT group posting a loss of £3.7 millions for the year. The new Challenger would have to work miracles

to justify such faith. It failed to do much at all and finally appeared at Brands Hatch at the end of 1975, when Dave Croxford was brought down in a first-bend melee. It appeared the next day with Scotsman Alex George in the saddle, but boiled over and stopped.

For the Challenger engine to be accepted for Formula 750 racing, it had to be proved that it was based on a production road unit, and a Commando with a road engine was in development. Dave Rawlins rode it at a very early stage and was not impressed: "Not any better than a normal Commando," is his opinion. To convince the FIM, motorcycling's international authority, that production of Challenger road bikes was planned, 25 Commando chassis with Challenger motors were lined up for inspection at Andover. "It's a good job he never touched any of them, or the engines would have fallen over," is the memory of team-man John MacLaren. The units had been borrowed for the occasion and simply balanced in place for the inspection.

NVT: the last rites

Events, however, overtook any racing plans. The Commando was offered with an electric starter in April 1975, but the installation of the Prestolite unit never did prove capable of turning the big twin over on a cold morning. Suggestions that it was really to assist the process were laughable when Honda owners had long been thumbing their starter buttons and getting an immediate response. The Triumph factory at Meriden had rebeled at the idea of closure, and a bitter dispute and no production had cost NVT dear. Three-cylinder Triumph Tridents built at the traditional BSA factory in Small Heath were cleared at desperate prices in the American market, as low as $1,000 if a dealer would talk big numbers and prompt payment. In November 1975 NVT went into liquidation and all production was frozen; the remaining parts in the Wolverhampton factory were built as a batch of 1,500 bikes, but the Commando faded from view, and the last tangible evidence of Norton seemed to rest in a small development unit in Staffordshire, where the rotary engine was quietly being worked on.

But the Commando has risen like a phoenix from the ashes of disaster. The spare-parts service to support an estimated 100,000 owners around the world became a mainstay of the Norton operation until it was sold to the Andover Norton wholesale operation in 1992. The supply of parts is now so extensive that two enthusiastic dealers, Les Emery of Fair Spares in Brownhills, near Lichfield (West Midlands), and Mick Hemmings of Northampton, build brand new Norton Commandos to order and export them energetically. Emery has even solved the problem of getting the electric starter to work, and today happy owners press the button and get results. The Commando is not built in large numbers any more, but it is a desirable hand-built machine with charisma – the legend is still very much alive.

CHAPTER SEVEN

THE ROTARY

*T*he Rotary promised so much, a compact engine with few moving parts and no vibration. The Norton development originally started as a

Triumph project in the late 1960s and survived the death throes of the Norton Villiers Triumph group. It first went into limited production for police and military use, and only after financier Philippe le Roux took over at the head of the company was it built for general consumption. Its potential was enormous, but lack of investment stunted its growth.

DURING THE FINAL months of the Norton-BSA-Triumph conglomerate, Dennis Poore arranged for a small development unit to be opened at Lynn Lane in Shenstone, south of the cathedral city of Lichfield (West Midlands). He wanted work to continue on the Wankel rotary engine, for which the company held a licence, away from the turbulence and upheaval that accompanied the demise of the British motorcycle industry as a major force.

The rotary unit was first run in a motorcycle at BSA-Triumph's Umberslade Hall development center; at that time it was a single-cylinder unit in a BSA 250 chassis. A twin-cylinder version was built shortly afterward and underwent development as funds became available. In 1976

▶ IT PROMISED SO MUCH, IT TOOK SO LONG TO DEVELOP, SO FEW WERE ACTUALLY MADE. THE 1974 ROTARY SHOW UNIT REFLECTED FIVE YEARS' WORK, AND IT WAS ANOTHER 13 YEARS BEFORE THE GENERAL PUBLIC COULD BUY A NEW MOTORCYCLE THAT WAS POWERED BY IT.

David Garside, an ex-Rolls Royce engineer with experience of rotary units, was moved to Shenstone and recruited freelance riders to put in road miles on the prototypes.

Logging the rotary mileage

One of the riders was Bob Rowley, working at the nearby Reliant car factory after Norton closed the Wolverhampton works; he would pick up a bike at 3.30 on Friday afternoon and return it on Sunday night with 1,000 miles added. Good high-mileage testing, but not of the bike in differing road conditions. When David Garside asked Bob what the rotary was like in traffic, the logical reply was: "Don't know. You're paying me for miles, and if I see traffic, I turn around and go in another

direction!" The contract was altered shortly after that conversation, so the testers got a fixed fee and instructions to try the bike in varying conditions.

Rowley rejoined Norton as a full-time inspector-cum-tester in 1979, and still has the logbooks he kept at that time. Filled in during lunch breaks at truck stops, they tell of the progress and problems of every one of the rotary units; number R2003's record indicates some of those problems, with seven rebuilds in its testing life and a note that the copper insert around the spark plug, intended to take heat away, was not working. The notes on other engines report problems with the housing cracking; machining expansion slots resulted in gas leaks, and the effect of filling the slots with a variety of adhesives had to be reported on after long, hard road miles.

Hele takes a hand again

In 1982 Dennis Poore contacted Doug Hele, then working as a designer at British Seagull outboard engines. "Apparently he was in trouble with the Wankel, and he wanted to put some pressure on the development side to overcome it," Hele explains. "We met at The Albany in Birmingham and went out to his car. Mr. Poore opened the trunk of the Mercedes to reveal all sorts of parts that he wanted to sort out." Hele, one of the greatest design engineers in the British motorcycle industry, was back in the fold.

"The police had development bikes on loan, and they weren't very happy with them," Hele recalls. "They were idling on one rotor, but at low speed in traffic they were cutting in on two. The Wankel has so little friction compared with a four-stroke poppet-valve engine that it's extremely difficult to get even mixture and smooth idling." It took years of careful experimenting (and very careful spending, because there was very little budget to support the work) to get the low-speed idling acceptable. "We had a stipulation that it had to do 3mph with the clutch engaged and then pull away,"

▼ THE FIRST PEOPLE TO BUY THE ROTARY WAS THE POLICE FORCE, WHERE RIDERS LIKED THE MODEL'S PERFORMANCE AND HANDLING, BUT FOUND IT TROUBLESOME WHEN RUNNING SLOWLY FOR LONG PERIODS. RELIABILITY WAS NOT REPORTED TO BE GOOD.

THOROUGH DEVELOPMENT WORK PRODUCED AN IGNITION SYSTEM THAT ALLOWED BETTER SLOW RUNNING OF THE ROTARY ENGINE. THE TRANSMISSION WAS BASICALLY THAT USED IN THE FIVE-SPEED TRIUMPH TRIDENT.

▶ THIS INTERPOL TWO WAS USED BY THE BRITISH TRANSPORT AND ROAD RESEARCH LABORATORY AS AN EXPERIMENTAL VEHICLE TO DEVELOP KNEE PROTECTORS THAT WERE THOUGHT TO BE ESSENTIAL AS A STANDARD ATTACHMENT FOR MACHINES IN THAT MARKET.

he explains. "The building at Shenstone is 217 feet long, so we used this to time ourselves, and if it took less than 48 seconds to ride that length it was wrong; if we took a minute, it was good. That's with the clutch engaged all the way." The final solution after long weeks of work on the carburation was an adapted Boyer Bransden ignition system that gave up to 50 degrees of retardation when the motor idled at just 800rpm.

By 1983 the factory had started selling machines to the police and had a water-cooled version under development. At its peak, active business was done with 30 different forces, but Norton remained shy

of publicity. It appeared to be unaware of the goodwill that the name still attracted and would fend off inquiries in a manner calculated to deter those who actually wanted to give their efforts positive publicity. There were numerous rumors of a civilian version of the model being launched, but years passed with no sign of rumor becoming reality. The police model was shown off to visiting parties, and the remarkable smoothness of the rotary engine was demonstrated by standing a coin upright on the fuel tank and revving the engine to the ignition cut-off point; the coin stayed upright.

Classic limited edition

In 1987 there were big changes at Norton. Dennis Poore succumbed to cancer, and the industry had lost a man whose contribution to its long-term future had sometimes been overshadowed by his abrupt way of dealing with delicate situations. The company now had the high-profile Philippe Le Roux at its head, and within a year there was tangible action when a limited edition of 100 Classics were offered to the public. At £6,000 they were not cheap, but all sold before the factory could finish building them: the famous old name still held magic for some. Bob Rowley tested every single Classic built and remembers that the first one despatched was Number 26, not Number One: "This woman nagged Philippe Le Roux to have it ready for her old man's birthday. We were

still working on the seat fixing, but Le Roux said 'Get it done and get her out of my hair,' so out it went."

Le Roux could see good publicity in racing and agreed to let Brian Crighton develop a bike in his own time. An air-cooled police machine was the basis, and there were senior factory personnel who openly doubted the bright young man's forecast of 120bhp. "I remember him coming past my office, looking in and saying 100, 110, and then 115 as they got more power on the dyno, and I'm getting worried, trying to design a transmission to stand this," is how Bob Rowley remembers those first days. "And remember, we had to use the standard transmission casing to be homologated for racing. When he got the power to 130, Brian put it on the bulletin board in reception. There were some who didn't like that at all!"

Rotary record at MIRA

It was Rowley who rode the bike in its earliest trim at the Motor Industry Research Association banked track, lapping at 155mph, which is still the fastest motorcycle lap there. Through the speed trap he clocked 170mph. Three weeks later, Crighton's bike made its racing debut at Darley Moor, the bumpy airfield circuit in Derbyshire. Rider Malcolm Heath was third first time out, but in the second race the transmission, a development of the old Triumph Trident five-speed unit, gave way.

Rowley later talked to Le Roux about the transmission and was asked how much a new transmission would cost. "I said 'I don't know for sure, but about £20,000' and he just said 'Do it!'" The standard casing was enlarged to increase the distance between shafts from 1.2 to 2.7 inches to accommodate bigger-diameter gears. "I got the pattern made and all the machining done by a local engineering shop in five weeks," says Rowley. "Mind you, they were on double money if they got it done on time."

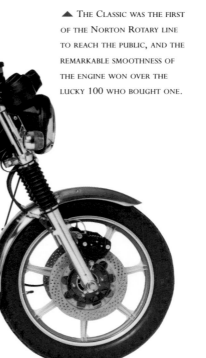

▼ WHEN PHILIPPE LE ROUX TOOK OVER AT THE HEAD OF NORTON AND DEMANDED PROMPT ACTION TO GET A CIVILIAN MODEL ON THE MARKET, THE AURORA MIGHT HAVE BEEN IT. BUT THIS ATTRACTIVE DESIGN WAS ABANDONED AND THE MOLDINGS THROWN AWAY.

▲ THE CLASSIC WAS THE FIRST OF THE NORTON ROTARY LINE TO REACH THE PUBLIC, AND THE REMARKABLE SMOOTHNESS OF THE ENGINE WON OVER THE LUCKY 100 WHO BOUGHT ONE.

1987 588CC NORTON CLASSIC

In 1987 the long-promised rotary-engined Norton for the civilian market was announced. A batch of 100 Classic models priced at £6,000, quickly sold out. The Classic used the air-cooled engine, and the running gear included one of the best rear-chain enclosures ever put on the market.

Test machines using this transmission had covered up to 90,000 miles on one chain, according to a factory spokesman at the time. Today the Classic is highly prized as a collector's machine.

ENGINE Air-cooled 588cc twin-chamber rotary. Compression ratio 7.5 to 1, twin SU HIF4 carburetors. Claimed power output 79bhp @ 9000rpm.

TRANSMISSION Primary by enclosed roller chain with hydraulic tensioner: secondary by enclosed roller chain, via 18-plate diaphragm clutch. Five speed transmission.

FRAME AND SUSPENSION Main chassis monocoque box section, telescopic front forks, and twin Koni dampers to swinging fork rear suspension.

WHEELS Cast alloy, front with 100/90 x V18 tire, rear 110/90 x V18.

EQUIPMENT Dual seat; speedometer; tachometer; warning lights.

PERFORMANCE Maximum speed approx. 130mph (208km/h).

DIMENSIONS Wheelbase 58.5in (1490mm); ground clearance 6.5in (165mm); overall length 85.5in (2172mm); handlebar width 28in (711mm).

WEIGHT 498lb (226kg).

PRICE £5,995.

The racing rotaries

In 1988 the serious racing effort began. The motors were mounted in alloy Spondon chassis, and a succession of star riders appeared on the wailing Nortons that were faster each year and thrilled the British crowds with a proud local name at the head of the field. Trevor Nation was one of the favorite jockeys, and gave the team Isle of Man success with second place in the 1990 Senior TT; he then finished third in the 1991 Formula 1 TT, only to be disqualified for using an oversized fuel tank. Riding in the distinctive black and gold John Player Special livery, Nation and team-mates were a stunning sight as they powered past the opposition with the full power of the rotary.

Robert Dunlop, one of the TT-winning Dunlop clan from Ireland, won the 1990 North West 200 – the Portrush, or Port Stewart circuit – and was clocked through a speed trap at 189mph – by far the fastest machine on the course. He followed

that up with third place in the Formula 1 TT, but a fall early in the 1991 season left him too weak to get the best from the Norton that year.

Ron Haslam, one of Britain's very finest, joined the team in 1991 and brought the *Motor Cycle News* championship alive with a series of slow starts and thrilling rides through to the top three places. But even Haslam and the Norton couldn't overcome that self-imposed handicap to win the title, and he ended the series in fourth place. At the 500cc British Grand Prix, he rode the new NRS588 to 12th place, after the FIM (Fédération Internationale Motorcycliste) agreed that the rotary could be allowed in on this occasion. In view of the earlier debates, when the Norton was said by some to be 588cc and by others 1176cc, it was a remarkable change of heart from the sport's international governing body.

◀ RON HASLAM, ONE OF THE FINEST DEVELOPMENT RIDERS AND AN EXPERIENCED GRAND PRIX COMPETITOR, WAS RECRUITED TO THE TEAM IN 1991 AND THRILLED BRITISH CROWDS WITH A SUCCESSION OF RIDES THROUGH THE FIELD FROM SLOW STARTS.

▲ STEVE HISLOP STUNNED THE SPECTATORS IN THE ISLE OF MAN WITH VICTORY IN THE 1992 SENIOR TT, USING ALL HIS GREAT SKILL AND CIRCUIT KNOWLEDGE TO GIVE THE COMPANY ITS FINAL VICTORY OVER THE FAMOUS COURSE.

TT glory once more

True glory came in 1992, when John Player's support was restricted to short-circuit events and other sponsors had to be found for the TT. With multiple Isle of Man winner Steve Hislop hired for the event, Norton found sponsorship from Abus Locks, and the red-haired dynamo from Hawick (home of Jimmy Guthrie, who had done so much for Norton more than half a century before) rode a rotary in unfamiliar livery. In the Formula 1 race, he was second to Phil McCallen, but a lap at 123.3mph made it clear that he was a major contender for the Senior race. On that day Hislop rode the Norton to the edge of its enormous performance ability, on the world's most demanding race circuit, in an epic battle with Carl Fogarty's Yamaha. At the end, the Yamaha had faded, and the Norton took the win by 4.4 seconds with a new race record speed of 121.28mph. And so, 85 years after Rem Fowler's victory in the first twin-cylinder race, a twin-cylinder Norton had won again.

There were a number of models offered to the public at this time, most notably the water-cooled Commander, a fully-faired touring model launched in 1989. To recognize the success of team member Steve Spray in winning the British Formula 1 Championship, the RCW588 F1 Replica was announced in 1989. In John Player Special livery, promised stunning performance, but erratic warm-weather running let it down badly. "After a speed run there would be a sudden loss of power," tester Rowley explains. "The fuel temperature was too high because it was all enclosed, and the hot air from the single radiator was affecting carburation. We tested the prototype in the winter, and there was no problem because that had twin radiators outboard of the carburetors. We raised the carbs on long inlet tracts so the float bowls were above the radiator, but it wasn't a complete cure." At a list price of £12,000, customers expected better than that.

THERE HAVE BEEN FURTHER RACING SUCCESSES FOR NORTON SINCE THAT 1992 SENIOR TT, BUT THE VICTORIOUS MACHINE IS A LANDMARK IN THE BRAND'S HISTORY AND HAS A DESERVED PLACE IN THE BRITISH NATIONAL MOTORCYCLE MUSEUM. HISLOP'S TT WINNING MACHINE DID NOT RUN IN JOHN PLAYER COLORS, AS THE TOBACCO COMPANY SUPPORTED THE TEAM'S CAMPAIGN ONLY TO WIN THE BRITISH NATIONAL CHAMPIONSHIP. ABUS LOCKS STEPPED INTO THE BREACH AND TOOK A PLACE IN TT HISTORY.

1990 RCW588 F1 SPORTSTER

The F1 was launched as a sports model, and to capitalize on the racing success of the John Player-sponsored team, it was available only in traditional JP black and gold livery. In prototype form it proved to be very fast, but when fitted with the sleek bodywork that gives it such visual appeal, there was not enough room for the twin radiators that the testers had been using. The result was a rapid build-up of heat within the bodywork and carburation that quickly went out of tune, to the extent that the bike would sometimes refuse to restart after a hard run. There have been few machines that look as good as the F1, and in years to come, it will be a collector's item to treasure.

ENGINE Liquid-cooled 588cc twin-chamber rotary. Compression ratio 9:1. Twin 1.3in (34mm) Mikuni BDS34 downdraft carburetors. Electronic inductive discharge ignition.

TRANSMISSION Primary by twin simplex roller chains with hydraulic tensioner; secondary by O-ring chain, via hydraulic wet multi-plate clutch. Five-speed constant-mesh transmission; ratios 2.571, 1.778, 1.381, 1.174 and 1.037 to 1.

FRAME AND SUSPENSION Aluminum alloy twin-spar beam frame. White Power upside-down front forks with adjustable compression and rebound damping; single White Power adjustable shock-absorber at rear.

WHEELS Front 17 x 3.5in (432 x 89mm) three-spoke cast aluminum; rear 17 x 5.5in (434 x 140mm) three-spoke cast aluminum. Front tire 120/70 ZR 17 ultra-low-profile tubeless radial; rear tire 170/60 ZR 17 ultra-low-profile tubeless radial. Front brake twin 12.6in (320mm) floating Brembo disks with 4-pot opposed-piston calipers; rear brake single 9.1in (230mm) Brembo disk with 4-pot opposed-piston caliper.

EQUIPMENT Single seat; streamlined fairing; speedometer; tachometer; temperature gauge; warning lights.

DIMENSIONS Wheelbase 56.7in (1440mm); ground clearance 6.9in (175mm); seat height 29.5in (750mm). Fuel capacity 5.3gal (20l); oil capacity 0.6gal (2.4l).

WEIGHT 423lb (192kg).

POWER 95 PS DIN at 9500rpm.

PRICE £12,500.

The 1990 range

At the 1990 Motor Cycle Show, a proud Norton display included a water-cooled version of the Classic, and the factory offered racing units based on the successes of past seasons; with carburetors, the price was £12,500. The F1 was priced at £13,900, and a new JPS Special version was a cool £15,400. Among the rotaries was a perfect replica of a 1962 500 Manx, built by Bernie Allen from current spares stock to confirm the excellent service backing Norton tradition. But the Show was hit by freak weather, the company received very few orders, and by Christmas they had laid off 25 of the Shenstone staff and production plans were under review.

For 1992 the F1 Sports was announced, priced to sell at £8,999, and there was an up-rated Interpol for police forces who wanted smooth engine performance. But there were financial problems: dealings in the company's shares were suspended, a Department of Trade and Industry investigation of the Norton Group's operation was under way, and a restructuring of the £6,000,000 debt to the bank was needed to make day-to-day funding available.

A new model was promised for the Motor Cycle Show, and the F2 was there to be admired for its sleek styling job. But none have been delivered and avid rotary enthusiast Frank Westworth, editor of *Motorcycle International*, says the machine shown had no engine internals! "I saw it when I went to the factory for a service and had a ride on it – they pushed me around the yard," he says.

As Norton changed hands and its problems continued, the racing team concentrated on the 1993 season and welcomed Colin Seeley aboard as team manager. Seeley has a reputation as a perfectionist, and in return for the support of Duckhams Oils, he turned out the most stylish team on the British racing scene. The pit workshop was carpeted and regularly vacuum-cleaned, and the rest of the Norton crew worked from that

standard up. Flying Scotsman Jim Moodie was recruited to ride, to be joined at the end of the season by fellow Scot Ian Simpson; but cash restraints meant no entry for the Isle of Man TT. The premier British race series was the HEAT SuperCup, and by the third round Moodie was in race winning form; at the end of the season, he won both races at Mallory Park (Leicestershire) to secure second place in the championship.

Simpson takes the British crown

New recruit Simpson took over the team-leader role in 1994, with Phil Borley in support. Simpson rose to the occasion and ended the 1994 season as British champion, while Borley was third in the hard-fought title race. All this success was earned against a background of confusion at the Norton factory, where the airplane engine division was

sold off. This was followed by a shock announcement: there would be a batch of 100 motorcycles built, and then the rotary would be no more. These doubts about the future supply of parts from the factory ended the glorious run of Norton racing success: Colin Seeley and Brian Crighton announced that in 1995 they were to run the Honda Britain race team.

Frank Westworth has been an enthusiast for the Norton rotaries for years and has owned two Commanders. "I wanted to buy the very last Commander and offered to buy one, money up front, if they would give me a written guarantee that I'd get it," he explains. "They said they couldn't do it."

There is no clear future for the great Norton name as these words are written, but its history stands proud.

◀ THE SCOTS HAVE SERVED NORTON WELL, FROM JIMMY GUTHRIE'S EARLY TT SUCCESSES THROUGH TO IAN SIMPSON'S BRITISH NATIONAL CHAMPIONSHIP VICTORY IN 1994. THE RACING TEAM CLOSED ON A HIGH NOTE, BEATING THE JAPANESE MAKERS' TEAMS.

PICTURE CREDITS AND ACKNOWLEDGMENTS

8 Jim Reynolds; 9 EMAP Archives; 10 NMM; 11 t, l EMAP, r EMAP; 12 t, b EMAP, r B R Nicholls; 13 National Motorcycle Museum (NMM); 14 t, b Jim Reynolds; 15 l, r Jim Reynolds; 16 t NMM, b Jim Reynolds; 17 l NMM, r Jim Reynolds; 18–19 NMM; 20 EMAP; 21 EMAP; 22–23 NMM; 24 Jim Reynolds; 25 l EMAP, r Jim Reynolds; 26 l Jim Reynolds, r B R Nicholls; 27 NMM; 28–29 NMM; 30 EMAP; 31 Jim Reynolds; 32 Jim Reynolds; 33 EMAP; 34 NMM; 35 EMAP; 36 EMAP; 37 NMM; 38 l B R Nicholls, r Jim Reynolds; 39 EMAP; 40 Jim Reynolds; 41 l B R Nicholls, r Jim Reynolds; 42 NMM; 44–49 EMAP; 50 NMM; 51 l EMAP, r Jim Reynolds; 52 t, l EMAP, r B R Nicholls; 53 t B R Nicholls, b Jim Reynolds; 54 B R Nicholls; 55 NMM; 56 B R Nicholls; 57 t EMAP, m NMM, b B R Nicholls; 58 NMM; 60 t, l Jim Reynolds, r NMM; 61 NMM; 62 t Jim Reynolds, l B R Nicholls, r NMM; 63 NMM; 64–67 EMAP; 68 l B R Nicholls, r Jim Reynolds; 69 EMAP; 70 t NMM, b B R Nicholls; 71 t NMM, b EMAP; 72 B R Nicholls; 73 l Jim Reynolds, r EMAP; 74–75 NMM; 76 The World's Motorcycle New Agency; 77 NMM; 78 t NMM, b The World's Motorcycle News Agency; 79 l EMAP, r B R Nicholls; 80 l EMAP, r Jim Reynolds; 81 NMM; 82 B R Nicholls; 83 NMM; 84–85 NMM; 86 NMM; 88 EMAP; 89 l, b NMM, r Jim Reynolds; 90 t NMM, b Jim Reynolds; 91 NMM; 92 Motorcycle News; 93 NMM; 94 NMM; 95 Motorcycle News.

Quintet Publishing would like to thank the National Motorcycle Museum, Birmingham, for allowing us access to the collection for photography (NMM pictures © Quintet Publishing Limited); also thanks to Carl Rossner for loaning bikes for photography. Index by Sheila Seacroft.